Getting the job you want often depends on how
you present yourself in an interview. Too often
uncertainty and anxiety prevent the job applicants
from doing themselves justice – and as a result
they do not get the job. This book sets out to make
the job seeker better prepared. It shows you what
to expect in the interview; looks at typical
questions and tests; advises on advance preparation and includes hints on communicating
effectively. Interviewing is often badly done. The
emphasis in this book is on how to help *you*
project yourself: so that you put forward your
qualifications for the job positively, rather than
relying on the interviewer to deduce them.

The advice in this book is addressed to any job
applicant, but it is of particular relevance for
anyone with limited interview experience –
school and college leavers and those changing
jobs early in their career.

Facing the Interview

A Guide to Self-Preparation and Presentation

CLIVE FLETCHER

London
UNWIN PAPERBACKS
Boston   Sydney

First published in Unwin Paperbacks 1981

UNWIN® PAPERBACKS
40 Museum Street, London WC1A 1LU

British Library Cataloguing in Publication Data

Fletcher, Clive,
　　Facing the interview
　　1. Applications for positions
　　2. Employment interviewing
　　I. Title
　　331.1′28　　　HF5383　　　80-40946

　ISBN 0-04-380023-8

Set in 10 on 11 point Baskerville by V & M Graphics, Ltd, Aylesbury
and printed in Great Britain
by Hunt Barnard Printing Ltd, Aylesbury, Bucks.

For Briony

Acknowledgements

I would like to thank the following individuals for their invaluable comments and advice while I was writing this book: Dr Rowan Bayne of the North East London Polytechnic, Viv Barker of the Kent College for the Careers Service, John Churchill (formerly of George Allen & Unwin), Dr Vic Dulewicz of Standard Telephone & Cables, and Dr James Walker of the Civil Service Department. I am also indebted to two anonymous reviewers, a Principal Careers Officer and a careers teacher, for their helpful suggestions on earlier drafts of the book.

Contents

I

A Positive Approach to the Interview

THE WIDESPREAD USE OF INTERVIEWS FOR SELECTION

The interview is still by far the most commonly used method for assessing a person's suitability for a job. In the USA, it has been shown that 99% of companies use this technique when hiring staff, and the equivalent figure for Britain is much the same. Only in the case of some unskilled jobs do organizations seem to feel that they can afford to do without the interview. Reliance on interviews as a way of fitting square pegs into square holes does not stop there, either, as this same technique is widely used in making promotion decisions too. So most of us will have the experience of being interviewed – for places at college, for jobs, for promotions and so on – not just once, but many times. The whole direction of our lives may be altered by success or failure in an interview that can be as short as 15 minutes or as long as three hours. The outcome can be just as important to the organization concerned; if they make a bad decision, they may be stuck with an unsuitable employee for years. In view of the importance to both sides, it is reasonable to ask whether or not the interview is a good way of selecting people for jobs.

ARE THEY EFFECTIVE?

With countless thousands of interviews being conducted each year, it is not surprising to find that there have been many research studies aimed at finding out just how good interview judgements are. There are two basic approaches to this. The first is to see whether or not different interviewers who (separately) interview the same people come to much the same assessments of them. One of the earliest studies of this kind was done in the 1920s, and involved 12 sales managers each interviewing 57 applicants for jobs as salesmen. It turned out that there was very little agreement between the interviewers in respect of how they rated the applicants; for example, a man rated first (i.e. the best applicant) by one interviewer was rated 57th, last, by another. This early investigation was somewhat crude, but its findings have, in general, been supported by many later studies. The fact that different interviewers assessing the same applicants can, and often do, come to widely different judgements of them clearly indicates that the interview as it is normally carried out is a highly unreliable way of selecting people.

The second type of investigation in this field attempts to find how well interview judgements predict the actual job performance of the applicants selected. In other words, if you interview a number of people and select two, one of whom you think is barely acceptable but the other you rate as very good, does the one your interview assessment said was best really do the job better than the one you thought was a borderline case? This research on the validity of interview judgements unfortunately produces results no more comforting than the studies of agreement between interviewers. For example, an investigation to find out how well college interviews predicted final degree classification showed that as good (or perhaps, more appropriately, as bad) a result could have been achieved by simply picking the names and degree results out of a hat.

The unflattering picture of the value of interviewing

as a means of assessment that has emerged from research has not, it would seem, dampened the enthusiasm for the technique. It remains the principal selection technique despite the many adverse findings. We shall see later that much can be done to improve the quality of interviewing and possibly even of the judgements arising from it, but it remains at present a rather imprecise way of assessing people. Why, then, do intelligent people who know about the fallibility of the interview persist in relying on it?

WHY INTERVIEWS ARE STILL USED

There are a number of reasons why the interview retains its popularity. On purely pragmatic grounds, it is very easy to arrange and to carry out (unfortunately, it is all too easy to carry out *badly*, but not as easy to carry out well!) However, this is not the main reason for its continued use. More important is the fact that an interview provides information that is difficult or impossible to obtain in other ways, e.g. what the candidate's appearance is like, how he conducts himself in a face-to-face meeting, whether he expresses himself clearly and well when speaking, whether he seems pleasant and personable, and so on. Also, the applicants usually *prefer* to be seen; they dislike the impersonal approach of being assessed entirely 'on paper' as it were, and like to make some contact with the 'human face' of the organization. There is some point to this, quite apart from vague subjective reactions, and that is the opportunity presented by interviews for the candidate to ask questions about the job, conditions of employment and so forth. So both sides have a vested interest in the continued use of the interview, 'warts and all'.

HOW INTERVIEWEES CAN HELP THEMSELVES

Most organizations have no intention of giving up the interview as a way of choosing people, though they will use all sorts of devices to train and assist their interviewers in the hope they will do a better job of assessing people. Where does this leave the interviewee? (N.B. Throughout this book, the terms 'interviewee', 'candidate' and 'applicant' will be used interchangeably.) Must he just accept that the interview is an imperfect procedure and hope either that he is faced by a good interviewer or that he is just lucky that day? He certainly has to accept that the interview is imperfect, but he does not have to take a negative, helpless attitude towards his own role in it - quite the contrary. He should realize that since even the most experienced interviewers sometimes make mistakes (precisely what sort of mistakes we will look at in Chapter 3), he cannot afford to take a totally passive role in the interview and it will often be up to *him* to make sure that his aptitudes, abilities and qualifications for the job are put forward and noted in the interview. To be in a position to do this, the candidate needs to know what kind of thing to expect in interviews, how to prepare in advance and how to deal with the interview situation itself.

THE AIM OF THIS BOOK

People attending for interviews are frequently unaware of what sort of questions are typically asked and of *why* the interviewers ask questions of that sort. The interviewees are rather like students having to take an exam where they know what the subject is but have never actually been told the syllabus. Small wonder that many of them come out of the interview feeling a mixture of bewilderment, resentment and regret - regret at the feeling they did not put themselves across better, that they have not done themselves justice. The aim of this book is to avoid situations of that kind; in other words, it sets out to help you put your best foot forward in the interview. It seeks to achieve this by doing basically two things. First, it describes how and why interviews are used, who carries them out, the different types of interview likely to be encountered and the sort of questions asked. This should help remove some of the mystery and folklore that seem to shroud interviews and sometimes make people more nervous about them. Second, it gives detailed and structured guidance on preparing for the interview, conduct and self-presentation in it and self-review after it. This information should enable you to take a more positive and active role in the interview itself. Quite apart from helping you personally, it should help the interviewer make better selection decisions (i.e. the decision as to who gets the job): if you have a better idea of what to expect in advance, how to prepare for it and tackle it, you should be able to put across more useful and valid information than would be the case if you were answering the questions hastily on the spur of the moment.

WHAT THIS BOOK WILL *NOT DO*

This book does not give advice on how to 'trick' interviewers or on how to fake one's way through selection procedures. It is *not* intended to help an individual obtain a job irrespective of his merits for filling that job.

WHOM THE BOOK IS MEANT FOR

The book has been written mainly with those leaving school or college and seeking their first full-time job in mind, particularly those who are going for jobs where educational qualifications will be of some importance. The reasons for limiting its aims in this way are given below.

(a) This group of interviewees need help on interviews more than most, because they have so little experience of them. As they attend more interviews, so their competence in handling them increases up to a point – but by that time several important job opportunities may have been lost, never to return. The earlier this group can be given some help on interviews, the better.

(b) The kinds of interviews faced by this broad group of people are often fairly similar in many respects.

So what is contained in the following pages has been written with one specific (albeit large) group in mind. However, much of the information and advice given does in fact apply to interviews in general and is thus likely to be useful to many people outside the group I have mentioned.

THE WAY THE BOOK IS ORGANIZED AND HOW TO USE IT

Although we are chiefly concerned with the interview, two brief chapters have been devoted to consideration of the application form and the use of selection procedures other than the interview (e.g. psychological tests), which might be given along with it. The rest of the book concentrates on the interview.

To really understand the interview and what goes on in it, you need to have a glimpse of what it looks like from the other side of the desk – the interviewer's side. Chapter 3 tries to show how the whole thing looks through the interviewer's eyes. Chapter 4 looks at the different types of interview and how they are conducted, then reviews the kind of questions interviewers ask and explains why they ask them. Following that we have the core of the book, Chapters 5 and 6, respectively, dealing with how to prepare for the interview and how to conduct yourself in it. At the end of the book is a short chapter on reviewing your own performance in interviews. Clearly most people will concentrate on what is said about preparing for and dealing with interviews, but do *not* skip the other chapters. You should read through the book once and then re-read Chapters 5 and 6. Shortly before an actual interview you will probably wish to use the Interview Preparation Programme and Checklist provided in the Appendix (more about this in Chapter 5), and shortly after the interview the last chapter should be re-read.

One final word. The idea for this book arose from my own experience as a practising psychologist; many of the interviewees (particularly college leavers) I see have little idea of what seems to be expected of them and of how to deal with being interviewed. The information and advice given here rests largely on my experience as an interviewer, as a trainer of interviewers and (not unimportant) my experience as an interviewee. It is also based on psychological research studies of interviewing, where relevant; however, I have seldom made this research base explicit, as to do so would probably turn this into a rather different and possibly less readable kind of book.

2

The First Step

SHORTLISTING THE APPLICANTS

It is all very well talking about interviews and how to handle them, but there is the small matter of actually getting an interview in the first place. The first step will normally be filling in an application form. Now, even at the best of times there are usually far more applicants than there are vacancies for any particular job, and in times of high unemployment the situation is even worse. Most application forms are rather long – four sides or more – and when a lot of people apply this gives the organization concerned a bit of a problem. With numerous long forms to wade through, you could spend a ridiculous length of time arriving at a shortlist of the few best applicants. In order to reduce this task to manageable proportions, it is usual practice to sift through all the applications and reject all those that appear to be of lesser quality when judged on some basic standards. For example, if a job requires that the job-holder should have a good degree, then whoever is sifting the applications may start by simply picking out the applicants who have the best degrees of this particular bunch, and rejecting the rest; then he would go through the rest in more detail before drawing up a final shortlist for interview. This first sift of applications is often a rather arbitrary procedure; an application can even be dismissed at this stage on grounds of illegibility (not that it will be truly illegible – just more difficult to read than the average). So you cannot afford to be careless in the way you complete application forms, and the next section gives some guidance on completing them.

THE APPLICATION FORM; SOME ADVICE ON COMPLETING IT

The two main concerns are that the form be filled in neatly and *correctly*. First, read through the form carefully before writing anything on it. Then, write out the information you are going to put under each section of the form on a separate piece of paper; this will often bring any errors or uncertainties to light and prevent you having to start crossing things out on the form itself. This 'practice' part is particularly important if the form has sections on it which require you to compose some paragraphs, e.g. some forms ask you to write a short autobiographical sketch, or to list all the key events in your life and say why they are important. Having written things out in rough, give yourself a day or so and then come back to it, look through it all again and, if it still makes sense, copy it out on to the application form itself. Better still, get it *typed* out on the form if you can; this looks a lot neater and is easier to read. If you cannot get it typed, then make sure you write it as neatly as possible. Should your writing not be very legible, try printing your answers where appropriate.

When you have completed it, read through the finished form. Check that all the information asked for is provided and that the spelling is correct (both of which should be correct if you have given some thought to these matters in the first drafting stage). Also, check the dates given, for instance in relation to a series of starting and leaving dates for jobs or schools; are there any inconsistencies or unexplained gaps?

Most of what has been said so far relates to the presentation of the form, which is particularly important in reducing the danger of being disqualified at the preliminary sifting stage. The most important thing, however, is obviously the content of the application. When writing a first draft as suggested above, think about what you are saying and try to look at it from the point of view of the organization to which you are applying: how will the information given on the form be interpreted, and what are the sort of things looked for? The other point that needs to be borne in mind is that the form usually plays some part in deciding what will be talked about in an interview. So what you put down now, say in regard to your leisure interests (*see* pp. 40 and 54 in this connection), you may well have to discuss in more detail if you are given an interview. *Do* put down things you will be happy to enlarge on orally and avoid putting down things that you will have difficulty talking about (unless, of course, they have to be mentioned, such as jobs you were not good at but which have to be included in your employment history). Try to ensure that anything that might work in your favour is included – all exam passes, extra qualifications, sporting or other achievements, social or community work, special projects, part-time work done if you are a student, and so on. If the form provides only very limited space for you to give information of certain kinds, then make sure that the information most relevant to that job is included, even if there is little or no room for anything else (e.g. if the job was in the area of social services, and you had done some voluntary pastime work helping old people, it would make sense to give that prominence). Finally, keep your first 'rough' draft of the application form or (preferably) photocopy it. Then, if you get an interview you will be able to refresh your memory of what you wrote on it and think about the kinds of questions that are likely to arise from that.

REFERENCES

You will usually be asked, somewhere on the form, to give the names and addresses of people who will give you a reference. These references (two are generally asked for) may just be people who know you well and will vouch for your 'good character', or they may have to be people who have some knowledge of your ability and achievements shown in employment or education. Irrespective of which kind of referee is required, always contact them and seek their consent before you put their name down on an application form. Many people would be willing to act as referees but take mild offence (or worse) at having this fact taken for graned. Not only is it polite to ask, but you can at the same time tell them about the job you are applying for. Taking this further, you might suggest what things could be stressed in the reference that would help this particular application – but whether or not you go as far as this very much depends on how well you know, and get on with, your referee.

It is quite good politics to write to the people you ask references of even when you are not applying for jobs. Letting them know what you are doing and how you are getting on from time to time will make them feel much happier about providing references when the time comes: they are less likely to feel that you are just making a convenience of them. This is important, as writing a well-worded reference takes time, and if he has to do it several times for you, your referee needs all the 'encouragement' you can give him (and that includes letting him know afterwards whether or not you got the job, and thanking him for his help either way).

There is also the question of *who* to name as referees. Many people find they have little choice anyway, as there are only one or two people who can really comment on their performance at college or at work. If you are lucky, however, you might have a choice of several people open to you; this happens more and more as you get older, because you work with a greater variety of people over time. The main points to keep in mind when deciding who to ask are:

(a) How much prestige or influence does this person have?
(b) How well does he know your work and abilities?
(c) How well you get on with him?
(d) How relevant his knowledge of you is to *this* application?

The above points are *not* listed in priority; it is up to you to decide your own priorities on this. One problem that frequently arises is that you do not wish to give your present employer as a reference when applying for a job, lest the knowledge that you are looking around for something else should jeopardise your present position. If other referees are available, then this can obviously be dealt with; however, if you have had only one job, the problem remains. In this case, it is probably best to ring the organization you are applying to and ask them whether or not they would be willing to defer writing to your employer until after the interview (references are usually taken up only when a candidate is short-listed for interview). Then, if you have not got the job they will not bother to write, and if you have been provisionally accepted your employer will probably have the good grace to accept the situation. (Even if he does not, and writes a bad reference, it is unlikely to lead to a reversal of the interview decision.) Clearly, there is an element of risk in this strategy and you must balance this against whatever level of risk you see in admitting to your employer beforehand that you are looking for other jobs and asking him for a reference; the reaction to the latter is not always negative, and sometimes even produces incentives to stay!

SUMMARY

The main points of advice given in this chapter might be summarized thus:

Copy out the longer, free-written parts of the form

(in fact, preferably *all* the form entries) first on a piece of paper.

Emphasize the most *relevant* and the most positive aspects of your qualifications and experience in your answers.

Give yourself time to think over your intended answers to the form's questions before completing the form itself.

Make sure that you complete the form neatly (have it typed if possible).

Read through the completed form and check for errors (spelling, dates, etc.).

Keep a copy of the form and your answers to it.

Choose your referees with care.

Consult any people you are thinking of as referees and get their permission first.

Thank them and inform them of the outcome of your application afterwards.

3

Interviewers: Their Task and Problems

The aim of this chapter is to put you in the other person's shoes, to see how things look from the interviewer's side of the desk. Some of the apprehension people feel about interviews springs from knowing so little about them as a procedure. In the following pages we will look at who does the interviewing, the basic task that confronts interviewers and the problems involved. This should not only take away some of the mystery from interviews but also make you a little more confident about facing them.

WHO CARRIES OUT THE INTERVIEW?

The person you face in an interview may be there through accident or design. He may have been selected almost randomly to carry out the interview or he may have been carefully chosen because of his knowledge of the job that is vacant and of the kinds of skills that will be needed by whoever fills it. One thing is almost certain: the interviewer will not be chosen because he has a gift for assessing people; if such individuals exist, they are seldom seen in interviews. So he or she will be a fairly average mortal, a fact easily lost sight of (sometimes by both parties) in the interview itself. Most commonly the interviewer is either someone from the personnel department or is the person who will be responsible for the work of whoever is to be appointed. In larger organizations, which tend to spend more time and money on selecting people for jobs, the candidate may be interviewed by representatives of both personnel and line management functions. There is some research showing that personnel managers look for slightly different things in job applicants compared to what other kinds of managers seem to concentrate on, but these differences are not large enough to be worth worrying about.

If you are going for a really important job, the organization may even unleash a psychologist as well as the other interviewers on you! Most people find that a relatively painless experience, I should hasten to add.

The ability to judge others

Trying to assess the personality of another person on the basis of a brief meeting, like an interview, is extremely difficult. We have already seen (in Chapter 1) how different interviewers often come to widely different judgements about the same applicant. Our assessments of other people are influenced by many things, some of them quite irrelevant. A lot of psychological research in the 1950s was aimed at finding what were the characteristics of individuals who were good at judging other people. One of the main problems found during this research was that hardly anyone is good at making personality assessments of other people in general. Some people were better than others at gauging the character and temperament of certain groups of people (e.g. students, middle-class housewives, etc.), particularly if they themselves were members of the same group – but the search for a type of person who was good at summing up any other individuals at all was unsuccessful.

Experienced and inexperienced interviewers

Some interviewers find it hard to accept that simply

doing more interviews does not of itself make them better at judging others (a fact established by research). After all, most of us like to feel that we can get the measure of somebody given a reasonable chance to chat with them, and if you are doing this kind of thing all the time (in the form of interviews) there is an understandable tendency to think that you are pretty good at assessing others. This occasionally gets taken to extremes by interviewers who claim that they can 'sum a man up as soon as he walks in the room'. Such claims tell us more about the person making them than they do about the interviewees, but fortunately one does not encounter that kind of ill-found arrogance very often.

If the amount of interviewing he has done makes no difference to his basic ability to assess people, does the experienced interviewer have anything else going for him? Well, experienced interviewers are usually more confident and have a better idea of what questions they want to ask – the result being an interview that moves along more comfortably for both sides and which will probably yield more information than an interview given by an inexperienced person. Unfortunately, without proper training there is quite a chance that the information obtained will be irrelevant to the selection process; and even with such training and useful information elicited in the interview, there is no guarantee that an experienced interviewer will actually *use* the information better in making his decision on who to appoint.

Inexperienced interviewers are usually easy enough to spot. Their lack of confidence shows in stammering, hesitancy and other aspects of the way they put their questions. Sometimes they bravely try to cover up with excessive casualness – like one interviewer I heard ask a candidate 'Are you married at all?' – to which the candidate would have been justified (but unwise) in replying 'Only a bit' or 'Yes, sometimes'. Quite often they dry up in the middle of an interview because they have not prepared properly or simply cannot think of what to ask next. This nervousness has an unsettling effect on some interviewees, and they lose confidence too, though some seem to relish the situation and more or less take control of the interview. However, generally speaking you are better off in the hands of an experienced interviewer, particularly one who has been properly trained.

The interviewer as a public relations officer

An organization will of course short-list for interview quite a few more applicants than it has vacant jobs. So for every 100 people taken on, maybe 300-400 will be rejected following an interview. This may be the only time that those rejected applicants will have face-to-face contact with a representative of that organization. If the interview was badly conducted, or seemed unfair, or if the interviewer treated the applicant less than politely, then the rejection will just add insult to injury. Any organization that is conscious of its public image will want to avoid that situation – it does not want a lot of disgruntled interviewees going round giving it a bad name. So the interviewer, if he is any good, will always be conscious of his public relations role and act accordingly (though this is not much more than he should do through good manners anyway). This is also a point that the employing organization should keep in mind when choosing who to do the interviewing for it.

MATCHING PEOPLE AND JOBS

It would be impossible to select people for jobs effectively without knowing a good deal about the jobs themselves. A thorough description of the job, the duties it involves and the circumstances under which it has to be done is required. When this information is available, in the form of a job specification, one can start thinking about the kind of abilities, qualities and experience that will be required to do it properly. This may lead to an idea of what an ideal candidate might be like; it is highly unlikely that any candidate will be wholly ideal, so there should be a list of priorities giving the most important and the least important (i.e. those which are essential and those which are just desirable) of the qualities wanted which will help decide which of the job applicants seems the most suitable.

Job specifications are very useful for getting clear in the interviewer's mind just what it is he is looking for. However, sometimes it is difficult to draw up a precise specification because people are being recruited to a general group of jobs, e.g. an executive officer in the Civil Service might be called upon to perform a variety of very different tasks at various stages in his career. Similarly, graduate management trainees entering large organizations are often given experience of numerous kinds of work before settling down to one main field. In these instances, the job specification will be expressed in much more general terms and selection will probably rely heavily on academic qualifications and the candidate's ability to convey a favourable impression of his personality in the interview. The interviewers are looking more for potential rather than an existing set of skills, which makes their task considerably harder.

So, with varying degrees of precision, the interviewers will know what information they need to get from applicants to assess their suitability for the job as specified. We shall see in Chapter 4 how they go about collecting that information and the kind of interview plans they use. All that we need to note here is that they will use a number of different sources of information, including references, academic qualifications, work experience and performance in the interview.

The matching process is a two-way affair in most cases; the applicants for a job will be seeking further information about it in the interview to make sure it is broadly what they thought it was and thus suitable for them. Quite often applicants find out things about the job in the interview that lead them to reject it when offered. This opportunity for the candidate to get further details and check on terms etc. is an important part of the selection process and emphasizes again that interviewees should not be thought of as passive elements in the selection situation. However, most applicants do decide they want the job and so the final decision rests with the interviewer. How does he make up his mind? If he has carried out his task properly, he should have on the one hand a job specification telling him what he needs, and on the other an assessment of each of the applicants he has seen on those attributes required. He then has to match the two sides together and see who fits the job specification most closely. That might seem simple, but is often anything but easy. For example, if the job specification lists three qualities or qualifications A, B and C in order of priority, the interviewer may find at the end of the day that he has one candidate who was excellent on A and moderate on B and C, another who was excellent on B and C but only moderate on A, and a third who was good, but not excellent, on all three. Which would he choose? Under such circumstances all sorts of personal factors might tip the balance in favour of one of the three, but the main point is that even with a systematic approach to selecting people the final decision does not get reduced to a mathematical exercise - the decision is often extremely difficult and influenced by all sorts of factors, both relevant and irrelevant. We will look at some of them later in the next section.

THE PROBLEMS INVOLVED

Carrying out a good interview is far from easy, carrying out a bad one is all too easy. In this section we will look at the kind of problems interviewers have to deal with and overcome if they are to do their job properly. A knowledge of these problems should help you understand what goes on in the interview and give you a better chance of dealing with it. It might even make you more sympathetic toward the interviewers!

The constraints on the interview

Time is the most obvious constraint; in most selection procedures several or all of the applicants have to be seen on one day, with each allotted a fixed time period. So the interviewers are generally working against the clock, which makes it all the more imperative that they use that limited amount of time to the maximum effect. Good interviewers will have worked out in advance the sort of things they want to talk about and will have planned the interview time accordingly. The less effective ones will frequently run out of time when they have covered only half of what they intended or, in some cases, will dry up half way through the interview.

A very different and fundamental constraint on the interview is that there is relatively little one can do to find out whether or not the interviewee is being truthful. Paper qualifications etc. can be checked, and references may provide further evidence on some things, but most of the other information has to be taken on trust from the interviewee. Skilful interviewing and observation of the interviewer's behaviour will often reveal some exaggerations or even downright lies (e.g. when someone claims to have a deep knowledge of a particular subject and when questioned on it appears to know little or nothing), but a great deal of what is said by interviewees remains unverifiable – it is their subjective response. This is something an interviewer just has to live with.

Getting the interviewee to talk freely

Even people who are confident and self-assured at other times can be nervous when being interviewed, and this presents interviewers with one of their most common problems. The trouble is that when an individual is tense, he tends to say less, to be hesitant in answering, to be less open about himself and generally to be less communicative (although there are some who react the other way by talking all the time as a way of trying to stop the interviewer from asking questions). This is bad from the interviewee's standpoint because he feels uncomfortable and gives a poor impression of himself, while from the interviewer's position he finds out little more about the interviewee than the fact that he is nervous in interviews. Some people might say 'Well, fair enough – he cannot face pressure so we will not employ him'. That, however, is a dangerous line of reasoning. A whole career may depend on an interview, and there are not many more important (and thus possibly anxiety-provoking) occasions than that; certainly everyday work situations seldom generate anything nearly as important to the individual, and nothing that he will get quite so charged-up about. So reactions to being interviewed should not be taken as altogether typical of how the individual faces stressful situations. And even if it is, the interviewer should ask himself whether the successful applicant will really be doing a job in which coping with stress is important anyway.

Bias

Why is it that different interviewers seeing the same person so often come to different assessments of that person (as in the study of salesmen mentioned in Chapter 1)? It could be that they started out with different ideas of what they were looking for, or that they asked different questions. Often, however, the reason for such varying assessment can come down to fairly simple old-fashioned prejudice or bias. We all have biases of some sort – things about other people that set our teeth on edge. Interviewers are no exception – they have their pet hates as well. Some of the things I have heard interviewers say they found objectionable about applicants include biting fingernails, chewing gum, chain smoking, not looking you in the eye, shifting in the chair too often, making too many hand gestures, fiddling with pens or other objects in their hands, tapping feet.

Quite a few of these are clearly unreasonable things to hold against somebody, particularly in the context of an interview. But biases are not necessarily rational –

one interviewer disliked candidates who had 'short arms' or acne! Indeed, it is all too common to find that people have prejudices based on physical characteristics. What can be done to offset the effects of such biases - which are after all irrelevant to the job (except possibly where the successful candidate is going to be working closely with the interviewer)? Unfortunately, very little. The important thing is that interviewers be aware of this danger and, through training or otherwise, identify their own particular biases. Even then, research has suggested that this does not always stop those biases operating.

From the *interviewee's* standpoint, the only way of not falling foul of interviewer's biases is to look at the examples cited earlier and try to avoid doing those sorts of things in interviews. However, more of that in Chapter 6. For the moment it is sufficient to note that personality judgements generally are fraught with difficulty and subject to many distorting influences. I have mentioned here just two that are of particular importance in the interview, but there are numerous others.

Other pitfalls of interviewing

One study of interviewers selecting personnel for the Canadian Armed Forces showed that the majority of the interviewers were, in effect, making their minds up about candidates within the first four minutes of the interview. This in itself is bad enough, as not only was there insufficient time to gather adequate information on which to base a decision, but the interviewers were often making their judgements on irrelevant information as well. However, the interviewers in this study seemed to form an initial impression of the candidate and then sought information which was consistent with that initial impression. Other investigations have thrown up the same kind of observation, i.e. that the interviewer decides to accept or reject the candidate early in the interview and then - largely unconsciously in all probability - conducts the rest of the session in such a way that he collects or perceives only that information which supports the judgement he has already made. The danger of making up one's mind about an applicant very early in an interview, and of the whole thing then becoming a self-fulfilling prophecy, is very real. As Dr Johnson said, 'God Himself, Sir, does not presume to judge a man until the end of his days.' As mere mortals, interviewers should have the decency and humility to wait to the end of the interview before judging an applicant. Fortunately, quite a lot of them do.

The commonest pitfall of interviewing is the poor phrasing of questions. Much of what interviewers get out of candidates depends on their asking the right type of questions. If they use 'closed' questions, i.e. questions that simply require 'yes' or 'no' or other equally brief answers, they will take a long time to get a little information. One often hears this type of question combined with the unfortunate and time-wasting habit of reading the application form to the candidate at the beginning of an interview:

'You went to X school?' – 'Yes'
'And you got Z qualifications there?' – 'Yes'
'After that you went to Y college?' – 'That's right'

Closed questions are inevitable sometimes and they do have their place, for example with candidates who are very unresponsive and despite encouragement offer little information about themselves. In such instances, a lot of closed questions might have to be asked. This is getting information the hard way. I fondly remember one interviewer who had to talk to a candidate about her leisure interests. Unfortunately for him, the candidate was a girl of 19 whose only interest was motor-cycles; she was something of a tom-boy and like her four brothers was 'bike-mad'. The interviewer, knowing nothing about motor-bikes or the culture associated with them, desperately tried every interest he could think of to try to get something to talk about, culminating in the ludicrously unlikely closed question 'Do you ever get together as a family and play Ludo?'

Interviewers should try to use open-ended questions that afford the candidate the opportunity to say a lot more than just 'yes' or 'no' in reply. So, instead of asking 'Did you join the dramatic society at college' they should ask 'How did you spend your leisure time when you were at college?' - or something along those lines. The whole point of such questions refers back to the problem mentioned earlier of getting people to talk in the interview; it is very helpful if questions are asked in such a way that they are invited to say a lot, that they have to say more than just 'yes' or 'no' to. When they do answer at some length, they will often produce leads which the interviewer can follow up with narrower, more detailed questions.

Another mistake interviewers are prone to make is to ask leading questions, i.e. those that give the interviewee a clear indication of the answer he should give. Sometimes this is quite blatant: 'This job calls for the ability to plan; do you like planning?', to which any candidate in his right mind will answer 'Yes'. On other occasions, the leading question betrays the interviewer's own beliefs and expectancies with varying degrees of subtlety, like the senior public servant I heard ask of a candidate 'What do you think of the way Nixon is being pilloried by the Press over this Watergate affair?'

There are numerous other mistakes one can all too easily make in phrasing interview questions, and we shall see more of them in Chapter 6 when we consider the best ways of dealing with each type.

Interpreting and using the information obtained

When interviewers have grappled with all these problems, with varying success, they come up against what is the final and possibly the biggest problem: how to use the information they obtained to make a (hopefully, correct) decision. They have some factual

.information on the candidates, and a great deal of subjective information based on their interview impressions. This will all vary in terms of its relevance and importance to the task of accepting or rejecting people. Part of the problem is that any interview conducted reasonably well can provide the interviewer with too much data. All human beings have limited information-processing capacity; that is, they can use only certain limited amounts of information to any effect over a given period. Trying to itemise all the information obtained, weigh it up and combine it to come to a selection decision probably is too big a task for our information-processing capacity to handle. A look at the complex research on this aspect of interviewing is beyond the scope of this book, but, in general, it shows that interviewers have to over-simplify the decision process as a way of keeping the task manageable. This involves all sorts of things, like sometimes giving much more weight to anything negative about the interviewee than to anything positive, using only part of the information available (which is what we see when interviewers make up their minds too quickly) and so on.

Quite apart from the strategies interviewers employ - largely unconsciously it should be said - to arrive at a decision, there is the immense difficulty inherent in the nature of the decision or judgement they have to make. In effect, they are trying to predict the future. They are being asked to say whether the individual they have briefly met will be able to take on at a later date a set of duties and perform them well. Not only that, but they are often required to pick people who have potential for development, who are going to be capable of doing many more senior jobs in time to come. When one remembers how much people and circumstances change over time, the difficulty of the interviewer's task is clear. All they have to go on is the impression they have of the candidate as he is here and now, and a past record of educational or other achievement. Neither past nor present performance are particularly good indicators of how well people will perform at higher levels in the future.

So both the process of coming to a decision·on selecting an applicant, and the kind of judgement being made in that decision present great difficulties for the interviewer. If he has tried as hard as he can to carry out his task well, he deserves your understanding of his problems, even if you do not always agree with the decisions he makes! And just in case you think that this is all an excuse to cover up for the mistakes interviewers make, here is some cold comfort for you. The decisions doctors make are subject to the same kind of information-processing limitations as those of the personnel interviewers, with rather similar results. For example, one study had an experienced group of medical practitioners examine stomach X-rays of patients with gastric ulcers and decide in each case whether the ulcer was benign or malignant. Broadly speaking, there are seven major signs that can be looked for in an X-ray to help make this particular diagnosis, and these signs are related to each other in a complex way which should be taken account of in making the diagnosis. The study revealed that the doctors just could not handle the complexity of this decision task and that they simplified it in much the same way as interviewers do. No doubt partly as a consequence of this, the doctors often disagreed with one another in their diagnosis. This is no isolated finding; there is plenty of other evidence (for example, the fact that around 80% of appendectomies are found to be unnecessary) to point to the difficulty medical practitioners have in making decisions even on the basis of relatively objective evidence. The personnel interviewer, working with little objective evidence and a great deal of subjective impression, has an even harder task; but at least he has the comfort of knowing that his mistakes are unlikely to kill anyone!

WHAT YOU AND THE INTERVIEWER ARE ENTITLED TO EXPECT

When talking to people after they have come out of interviews it is apparent that many of them have little or a wrong idea of what they were supposed to expect. Some have the idea that they are supposed to be treated like glass - fragile, handle with care, while others expect various degrees of interrogation up to a level not far short of the Inquisition. As a rough guide, you are entitled to expect the following:

(a) that you will be treated with courtesy
(b) that you will be given adequate opportunity to say what you want and that the interviewer will listen attentively
(c) that both your good points and your defects will be noted and taken into account providing they are judged relevant
(d) that you will be made to think hard and (often) quickly at some stages in the interview, e.g. when having to defend your viewpoint on a topic
(e) that the interviewer will withhold judgement on your application until the end of the interview
(f) that the interviewer will base his assessment of your suitability on information relevant to the peformance of the job in question.

In return, what is the interviewer entitled to expect of you? Basically that:

(a) you are serious in your application and thus about the interview itself
(b) you will be honest in your answers to any questions (providing they are fair), always allowing for some understandable distortions that creep in when people are talking about themselves
(c) you will be courteous and attentive
(d) you will be able to talk about anything you have indicated as being of special interest to you.

This does *not* extend as far as the case of one interviewer I remember. He was questioning a candidate who had seven years previously taken a fairly basic exam in economic and social history, which he used as justification to launch the following blockbuster 'How does Britain's joining the European Economic Community fit in with her social and economic development over, say, the last 250 years?' This is an essay question rather than an interview question and was totally unjustified - all the more so as the interviewer could not even answer the question himself, as I made a point of finding out!

4

The Way Interviews are Conducted

DIFFERENT TYPES OF INTERVIEW

There are two main types of interview used in selection, the one-to-one interview and the panel interview. These are described in this section. Both may be encountered in the same selection procedure, particularly in the more extended and sophisticated examples of such procedures. So you may be given a one-to-one interview first (as when employers visit the universities in the Spring each year on the so-called 'milk round'), which leads on later – if you make a good impression – to further sessions involving interviews of both types and possibly some psychological tests also. However, most organizations tend to use one type or the other, and do not mix them together in this way.

The one-to-one interview
This may also be called the individual interview, and as its name implies it consists simply of one interviewer talking with one applicant. It is the easiest interview to arrange and conduct, and in consequence is the type most commonly encountered. In particular, it is widely used in industry and commerce. The individual

interview has a number of advantages; apart from being relatively inexpensive to carry out in terms of man-hours, it is also generally felt to be a more relaxed approach that moves away from the tense formality often associated with panel interviews and instead becomes more like a guided conversation between two people. Moreover, if the interviewer is himself the person who will be supervising the work of the successful applicant, then both parties have an opportunity in the interview to size each other up and try to assess how well they would get on together (additionally, in this situation, the interviewer is particularly well-placed to answer the candidate's questions about what the job involves).

There are disadvantages to interviews of this kind, however. The main one is that it inevitably depends heavily on the personality and ability of one individual. If he is not a good interviewer, he may elicit the wrong kind of information, or perhaps very little information at all. Worse still, his own particular biases may determine who gets the job (though if the person who gets the post *is* going to have to work with him, it could be argued that for the sake of harmony this would be no bad thing). Again, in the case of more general posts where the individual may get moved around from one part of the company to another fairly often in the early stages, one interviewer may not be in a position to give a full picture of the work and answer all the questions on it.

In order to overcome some of these disadvantages, many of the larger organizations carry out sequential interviews, i.e. a series of individual interviews. The different interviewers may cover different topic areas in the interviews (if they do not, they are duplicating each other's efforts), and between them should be able to represent the interests of the various sections of the organization. With several interviewers pooling their judgements on a candidate, there should be less chance of the final decision being influenced by the particular prejudice of just one person.

The panel interview

Panel interviews are often referred to as board interviews. The panel or selection board may range from two to (in some absurd instances) 100 people, but usually consists of three to five interviewers who see the candidate together. This technique is particularly prevalent in public-sector bodies, such as the Civil Service, education authorities and so on. The reason for them using it is primarily so that 'justice can be seen to be done'. In other words, with a number of people carrying out the interview there is less chance of the applicant being treated unfairly as a result of single interviewer's particular likes and dislikes; each inter-viewer acts as a check on the others' judgement and the procedure as a whole is fairer. Though a cynic might suggest that four interviewers just means four times as many prejudices and an even greater likelihood of rejection on irrelevant grounds, the board interview probably does help control much bias and moderate extreme views (if conducted properly) and thus is clearly of particular importance for posts in public service.

There are other advantages of this kind of interview: it tends to be the opposite of the individual interview (i.e. the advantages of one are the disadvantages of the other, and vice versa). The panel interview allows for division of labour amongst its members: each member can concentrate on a different topic. It also means that while one member of the board is talking with the applicant, the others will be listening carefully for leads they can follow up when it is their turn to question him. The biggest single drawback to this approach is that it is difficult to establish rapport; facing a row of four or five people sitting the other side of the table is not particularly conducive to feelings of calmness and relaxation. So the panel interview tends to be a rather formal procedure. Some applicants actually prefer this and feel more at ease with the more formal situation, but one feels the majority do not. The less rapport one can establish with an applicant, the less easy it is to get him to talk freely in an interview. As in any interview, the individual's reaction to a panel interview depends in part on how it is conducted. If it is done well, the panel members will normally take it in turns to ask their questions of the candidate, and they will have agreed in advance what areas each one will cover. The first member may spend ten minutes questioning the applicant about his present and past jobs, the next one may spend a similar amount of time on education and qualifications, and so on. The alternative is a free for all in which any member of the board can ask questions at any time. This bombardment of questions coming in from different directions is apt to be rather confusing for the candidate, and does nothing to help him relax. It is also an inefficient method since at the end of sessions conducted in this manner the panel members usually find a collection of topics they have failed to raise.

The key figure of an interview board is the Chairman. He or she has the job of organizing the board and its way of operating – often allocating the topics to be covered to the individual members of the panel, making sure that they do not overrun their time 'slots' during the interview, acting as link-man between each member as one completes his questioning and another starts, and taking charge of the overall assessment of the candidate after the interview. The Chairman will normally be the first person to greet the candidate when he enters the room and will probably ask the first few questions: it is his task to help the candidate settle down as quickly as possible. At the end of the interview, the Chairman will probably round off by asking a few supplementary questions (often ones that his colleagues have missed, or ones that arise from the candidate's previous replies), and then terminate the interview. Obviously, much will depend on how efficiently the Chairman controls his colleagues on the board; if he does it well, all will progress reasonably smoothly, but if he does not, a very awkward shambles of an interview will result.

A SYSTEMATIC APPROACH - SOMETIMES

Having looked at the two main types of interview, we can turn to the way the interviews are conducted. One of the best ways of improving the standard of interviewing is to adopt a systematic approach - an interview *plan*. This does not mean that the interviewer works out in detail everything he is going to ask beforehand and then puts his head down and ploughs through his list in the interview itself. All that is required in a planned approach is that he establishes in advance what information is needed, how it can be organized under different headings and in what order and style those headings are going to be used to direct the progress of the interview. There are a number of such plans in common use, probably the best known being Professor Alec Rodger's 'Seven-Point Plan'. Typically, the information to be sought might be classified under the headings of present job, education and training, previous work history, interests, and family background; the order in which these topic areas are to be tackled in the interview, and what things are to be covered in them should also be decided in advance, though in these respects the interviewer has to keep a degree of flexibility, so as to cope adequately with the inevitable variations between individual cases.

Most trained interviewers will work to a plan. The candidate may view this with mixed feelings. On the one hand, the kinds of things discussed in the interview will probably be easier to predict if a plan is being used, and the interviewer should cover all the relevant ground (so the candidate should have no complaint about important experience or attributes being ignored). On the other hand, if the interviewer is using his plan well, the interview will be a thoroughly testing one for the candidate - no easy ride!

This kind of systematic approach is still found only in a minority of cases - though an important minority, as it includes most of the interviews done for management trainee posts in the Civil Service and in large industrial organizations. The bulk of employment interviews continue to be done in rather haphazard fashion, the interviewers not having much idea of how they are going to tackle the interview. This makes things more unpredictable for the applicants; the interviewer may follow a line of questioning quite inappropriate for the assessment he has to make, and which nobody would have thought likely to come up in that instance. However, even allowing for the whims of untrained interviewers, much can be done to anticipate what sort of things will be asked and to prepare accordingly. Certain topics are dealt with in just about all planned interviews and many of them come up in less well organized interviews too (though the latter often neglect to gather any information at all on some topics); so we will now look at these most frequently encountered areas of questioning in some detail.

THE QUESTIONS ASKED, AND WHY

In this section, we will look at eight main headings under which interviewers are likely to seek information, give some examples of the kind of questions asked* and try to explain *why* they are asked. Different interviewers might categorize their topics to be covered in different ways to the one given here, but much the same information and kinds of question would be involved.

The amount of time given to each of these areas in an interview, and the importance attached to the information obtained on any one topic, will vary according to individual circumstances. For example, for a school-leaver, the topic of work experience hardly arises, while education and training as an area of questioning will probably take a significant slice of the interview. The other point that should be noted here is that these eight

* A much fuller list will be found in the Interview Preparation List, in the Appendix.

topic areas inevitably overlap one another, and that the distinctions between them are slightly artificial. The interviewer may split up his task under these headings for convenience, but he will attempt to integrate all the information and use it to gain a picture of the 'whole' person.

Family background

The sort of questions might include:

> 'What is your father's job?'
> 'Have you any brothers or sisters? Are they older or younger than you?'
> 'What work do they do?'
> 'What did your parents feel about you staying on at school to do "A" levels?'

Applicants are sometimes puzzled to encounter these questions, wondering what relevance they have to their own suitability for the job in question. There are a number of reasons for seeking this kind of information. An important one is to find out how well an individual has done in relation to the opportunities available to him or her. For example, a girl who gets a couple of 'A' levels with fairly modest grades and who does so against a background of financial hardship and lack of parental support or interest in her academic endeavours might well be adjudged to have achieved more than someone getting the same 'A' levels but coming from a comfortably-off family which also gave strong support and encouragement. This kind of assessment is clearly not an easy one to make, and the interviewers need to gather as much information as they can about the individual's family and their circumstances. The other point here is that with young job applicants, most of their lives so far have been spent in the context of the family and it can be expected to have exerted a vital formative influence on their personality and character (an influence that possibly does not decrease all that much even when they are older).

Family background and circumstances are two of the most important areas for an interviewer to cover if he is to get a full picture of the applicant, but ironically these matters are often missed out altogether or dealt with only very sketchily. The reason for this frequently turns out to be a reluctance on the part of interviewers to risk appearing intrusive. They often feel that asking questions in this area is a little like prying (which perhaps explains why questions like 'father's occupation' are sometimes asked on the application form rather than in the interview). This is unfortunate, since few candidates object to these quite straightforward questions, even if they are not always quite sure of the point of them. Nor is there much reason for them to object, as the information obtained in this area very seldom actually produces evidence *against* a candidate but often puts him in a better light.

Education and training

Some of the questions here will simply be aimed at obtaining factual information or clearing up queries over exam results and grades, courses taken and so on. Most of the basic information will already be available to the interviewer if you have had to fill in an application form. The rest of the questions are a little different and probably require more thought, for example:

'Why did you choose to do economics at university rather than one of the subjects you took at advanced level in school?'
'What did you think were the best features of your degree course? What were the weakest aspects of it?'
'What subjects did you like most at school? What did you like least? Why?'

With young applicants who have either no work experience or only a minimal amount, the interview often centres strongly on the individual's education. *What* he has done is usually known. *Why* he did it, what he felt about it and the influence it has had on his attitudes and aspirations is the further information required. This has a bearing on motivation (see below) and can also reveal, in talking about likes and dislikes, what he did best and worst at school or college – something about his work aptitudes and preferences that may be relevant to the position the individual is applying for.

The non-academic aspects of school or college life may also be covered; things such as societies or clubs belonged to, positions of responsibility or authority held within the school or college and so on. The usefulness of this kind of questioning is that it can tell the interviewer something more about you as a person, your experience and your attitudes.

The questions encountered under this topic tend to be similar irrespective of the kind of institution involved, whether it be school, college or some other place of training.

Work experience

Once again, the interviewer will probably have the main details of the person's work history outlined on the application form, and this will usually tell him where the individual worked, what the job title was and how long he was employed there. In order to assess the true relevance of this work experience to the post he is seeking to fill, the interviewer needs much more detail. So he should ask questions along the lines of those given below:

'You worked as an executive officer in the Department of Trade. What did this job involve?'
'What parts of the job did you like best? What parts did you like least?'
'What were the main problems you encountered in this work? How did you deal with them?'
'What were your colleagues like?'
'Why did you take the job in company X?'
'Why did you eventually leave company X?'

As will be gathered from this, the interviewer has to

find what duties were involved in the jobs the individual has done, and the implications that can be drawn about his ability to exercise responsibility, his supervising experience, the sort of training he has been given and so on. This will help the interviewer weigh up the extent to which an individual's previous jobs have contributed to his ability to do the one he is applying for now. The interviewer will also be interested in how the individual describes his colleagues and how he got on with them: is he likely to fit in here? The reasons given for taking and leaving jobs can also be very informative, often indicating what kinds of work the applicant has not been happy with or suitable for in the past. If he has been through a whole string of jobs, none of them lasting very long, the interviewer will very understandably want to know what the reasons are for such an unsettled work history.

With older applicants, previous work record is going to be perhaps the most significant part of the interview, because the type of work an individual has done before, and how well he seems to have succeeded in various aspects of it, are going to be the most reliable indicators of how well he would be likely to make out in the post for which he is now being considered. An applicant with a considerable amount of work experience will not usually be questioned thoroughly on all of it, as interview time is very limited, so the interviewer will often try to obtain the applicant's general views, preferences and attitudes regarding his previous employment and only go into detail on the most recent and/or most relevant jobs.

Although this area of questioning is not appropriate for school and college leavers, they may well have some vacation or other part-time work experience which attracts the interviewer's attention, in which case the kinds of question asked will probably be much the same as those given to someone in fulltime employment. However, the scope and intensity of questioning is generally reduced if it is concerned only with vacation jobs, as is the usefulness of the answers in predicting how well the individual will cope with a permanent job.

Motivation and aspirations

It has been said that people can be divided into those who work to live and those who live to work. This is doubtless an over-simplification, but it does highlight the very real differences in the way people feel about their work and the kinds of satisfaction it provides for them. The interviewer may want to probe this area. He will want to assess your motivation towards work in general and, in particular, towards the kind of job he has to offer. This, however, is a rather difficult task because of the more abstract nature of the factors he is trying to assess. It is not the sort of area where he would be likely to say, 'Well, now I would like to discuss your motivation and aspirations'. Most interviewers would fight shy of such a bold approach to the subject, besides which there are very few questions which relate specifically to this part of an interview. More commonly, an individual's motivation and aspirations are inferred from what he has said in reply to other questions on other topics. In particular, the reasons the interviewee gives for doing what he has done in the past (the decisions he has made in relation to education and work, and how those decisions were taken) may give some good pointers as to motivation and direction. There are some questions that can be put directly on this, e.g.

'Why have you decided to apply for this job?'
'Where do you see yourself in, say, five years time?'
'What sort of work would you most like to do, given a free choice?'
'What would you do if you inherited a large sum of money?'

The reasons for asking the first question are pretty clear, though the value of the answer is not at all clear; many people (if they have any sense) have prepared an answer for that if for nothing else, and sometimes it is an answer framed more with what it is thought the interviewer would like to hear than with the truth in mind! We will say more about this later.

What the individual's aspirations are is another concern. Is he a person who has a clear, set (perhaps too set?) idea of what he wants to do, or is he someone still making up his mind, or is he drifting along quite aimlessly? Are his ambitions realistic, too high or too low taking into account the scope of the job offered, the chances of progression in it and the evidence of this person's ability to date? The interviewer needs to get answers to all of these questions, and mostly by gathering his information indirectly. If he fails, he may find he has taken on someone who is going to be frustrated by the limitations of his post, or who will happily settle for a comfortable level of performance well below both what he is capable of and what is really needed. It can end up as an expensive and unfortunate mistake for either or both parties, you and the interviewer.

Leisure interests

Not always a feature of interviews, but quite common as a topic and one you should be prepared for. The range of questions is very large and will take any pastimes or leisure pursuits you have put down on the application form as the starting point. If no information on this has been asked for on the form or in any of the other papers then the interviewer will have to start from scratch:

'How do you spend your spare time?'
'Do you have any hobbies?'
'Do you play any sport?'
'I see you say reading is your main leisure activity. How many books do you get through each month? What do you get out of your reading? Have you a favourite author? Why do you like him in particular?'

The last series of questions is the sort of follow-up and probing the interviewer has to do to establish whether the interest is a deep or even a genuine one. Apart from the depth of your interests, he may also try to assess the range of them. Why? Quite a few candidates are asked questions about what they do in their spare time and think to themselves, 'What on earth has this got to do with whether I am the right person for this job? What business is it of theirs anyway?' Well, there is some point in asking about leisure pursuits. Firstly, it may say something about you as a person: do you, in general, go in for team or individual activities? Are your interests predominantly physical or intellectual? Do you take any part in organizing leisure activities?

Secondly, if you are talking about something you are interested in and presumably know about, it should offer the interviewer an opportunity to assess how well you can express yourself. Do you explain things clearly? Do you convey your enthusiasm to others?

Thirdly, the interests of an individual sometimes do (if he is particularly lucky) complement his work. And sometimes a keen interest in and obligations arising out of a pastime can be incompatible with the demands of a particular job (if it involves a great deal of travel, for example). So the interviewer will want to find out whether your interests (if any) are likely to supplement or supplant your contribution at work, or have no effect either way.

General topics

Again, this is optional in as much as it does not relate directly to your background, qualifications and so on. But some interviewers, mainly in the public service, ask questions on current affairs or social issues, such as:

'How do you think we should use the revenue we get from North Sea oil?'
'What are the arguments for and against the rapid development of nuclear power as an alternative energy source?'

Obviously, the questions will change according to the
issues of the day, though they will generally steer clear
of blatantly political or religious topics. If they do not,
they are liable to find unsuccessful applicants attribut-
ing their failure to get the job to the notion that the
interviewer's political or religious ideals differed from
their own (which could indeed be the reason if the
interviewer let the discussion on a topic degenerate into
a heated political debate).

But why ask questions on topics like the Common
Market, the education system or whatever? Well, firstly,
it is to see if you are aware of the world beyond your
front gate and what is going on in it - in effect, to see if
you take any interest in society as a whole. If you do
(and you certainly *should*) the interviewer may wish to
find the extent to which you are able to form and
express your opinions on topics. This is the second
reason for asking questions on general topics: to see
how well you can express your views, how articulate
you are in presenting your case (your abilities in this
direction will be important in many areas of work).
Allied to this is the third reason for covering this
ground, namely to see if you are any good at defending
your viewpoint on a topic. The interviewer will (if he is
good) take on the role of devil's advocate and adopt a
point of view opposite to your own simply to see how
effectively you can support your idea in the face of
opposition. Is the candidate going to stick to his guns
or will he collapse at the first sign of an argument? Has
he 'thought through' his position on this topic? Does he
know and understand the opposing viewpoint, or does
he only look at things from one side of the fence? All
these questions and more may be in the interviewer's
mind when he discusses general topics with a
candidate. Without any doubt, this can be one of the
most stressful and testing parts of an interview, and one
that really makes the applicant 'think on his feet'. It is
demanding for the interviewer too, and many of those
who ask questions of this kind do not make a very good
job of it - they simply get the candidate's views and

neglect to challenge them in any way. Others quite unfairly expect the candidate to know about any subject they choose to light upon, (all too often the interviewer's own pet interest). Some guidance on anticipating the kind of topics that are raised will be given in a later section (p. 56).

Specialist and technical matters

Clearly of importance in some jobs (mainly in scientific, technical or professional fields), some interviewers will concentrate quite heavily on testing specialist knowledge. A few go as far as to turn the interviewer into a kind of 'oral exam', but much more often this area of competence is assessed mainly on paper qualifications. However, there are a number of things that may induce an interviewer to test a candidate's specialist knowledge in the interview. It may be that the individual's paper qualifications are not all that impressive and he or she is a borderline case, so that any extra evidence on his or her technical expertise would be useful. More generally the motive might be to see how well an applicant can explain aspects of his or her subject orally, and, in particular, whether he or she can convey technical concepts and procedures in a way that a non-specialist is able to understand. The interviewer could also ask questions of a sort that would seek to discover whether a candidate had thought about the way in what his or her specialist knowledge related to the particular job applied for. This area is one more opportunity for the interviewer to get some idea of how quickly the candidate can think when placed under some pressure (as most candidates feel they are in the interview). One final reason for concentrating on technical topics in the interview is that these are the things the interviewer himself feels happiest talking about in some cases, as is often so with interviewers who are actually specialists in some area.

The range and type of questions on technical matters is vast and inevitably depends heavily on the field involved, so there is little point in trying to give specific examples here. The type of question that might come up (within the time limitations of an interview) will be apparent to the candidates in their respective fields, but note the advice given on p. 57. As a supplement to these questions, a candidate may be required to bring a workbook of projects or some other sample of work along to the interview to discuss.

Health

Very seldom do questions on the candidate's health come up. Other sources of evidence are used (either a note from the individual's physician, or a medical examination), or often nothing at all is asked on this. Application forms sometimes have questions relating to health, and if any incapacity or illness is declared on the form by the applicant he can expect that it will be followed up in the interview, should he get one. Some jobs clearly do require evidence of good health because of their physically demanding nature, but in these cases few interviewers would be sufficiently foolish to rest their assessment of an applicant's health on his own subjective opinion on it.

PUTTING THE PICTURE TOGETHER

Having asked questions in some or all of these areas, the interviewer has to assemble his information and come to a conclusion. He has been building up a picture of the applicant from the first moment of the interview. This picture is not just a series of headings under which he has collected information; it should integrate the information in a way that will help the interviewer imagine what the applicant would actually be like doing the job. He will be asking himself the sort of questions given below.

Does the applicant have a capacity for leading others?
Is he likely to be steady, and dependable?

Will he prove an acceptable colleague?
Has he sufficient (or even too much) self-confidence?

These are not things that can be asked directly in an interview, but will be inferred from answers given throughout the session. The other important part of the overall impression created is whether the applicant has come over as a personable and pleasant individual; in other words, does he seem to have an agreeable disposition? This has been shown to be of primary importance to some interviewers, which is perhaps not too surprising (though still mistaken) if one assumes that *all* the candidates shortlisted for interviews are acceptable in terms of their basic qualifications anyway.

We have looked at the types of interview you are likely to encounter, at the approaches taken to them, and at the main areas under which interviewers seek information. In the following chapter we will look at how this and other knowledge about interviews can be used in preparing for them. While doing this, it might be useful to keep in mind the reasons interviewers have for seeking the different kinds of information and to judge the sort of picture of you that they might build up from it.

5

Preparing for the Interview

GETTING PRACTICE

Practice helps performance in most things, and interviews are no exception. Practice can help interviewers *and* interviewees to improve their handling of the interview, particularly if it is practice under *guidance*. For the interviewers, this is no great problem because there are training courses they can attend where they will be given feedback on their performance as interviewers during practice sessions, usually supervised by psychologists. Such facilities are seldom available to job applicants, needless to say. There *are* some courses run at colleges that specifically aim to give feedback to candidates on their self-presentation in interviews, but these are few and far between. If the chance arises to go on a course of this kind, by all means take it. Perhaps the next best thing is to volunteer to act as a 'guinea pig' candidate on courses for training interviewers; they have to interview someone in their practice sessions, and often seek volunteers to take the role of job applicants for this purpose. Not only do the volunteers generally get paid but the tutors on the course will be able and willing to counsel them on their interview performance. So again, if the opportunity should arise, by all means volunteer - it will probably prove an interesting, valuable and even financially rewarding experience!

These two limited chances of getting practice are the best, but by no means the only ones. It may be that careers masters in schools or teaching staff in colleges can lay on some kind of practice sessions, with or without the aid of outside advisors (psychologists, personnel managers, etc.); if they do not do this at present and you would welcome such help, try asking to see if they have thought about arranging something of this kind. Practice without somebody being there to tell you the good and bad points of your 'performance' in the interview can also be useful, so you can get this practice by going for job interviews. Unfortunately, it is, of course, not very easy to get interviews and you cannot afford to treat them as just practice sessions when you do (unless it is a job you really do not want). Nevertheless, every interview provides some practice and if you review your own part in it as soon as possible afterwards, you can profit from the experience; this will be discussed in more detail on p. 92.

Practice is of enormous help, and if you are lucky enough to find one of the courses referred to above, then all well and good. For the vast majority, however, the best (and indeed, only) help that is available may be the kind of written guidance provided here, allied to their own experience of actually being interviewed.

FINDING OUT ABOUT THE ORGANIZATION

The organizations you apply to for jobs (in most cases) expect you to have some knowledge of the job in question and of the organization itself. This is not unreasonable, since to select and train someone is normally an expensive process; if the individual drifts into it without really knowing what to expect, he may very quickly find that it is not to his liking and leave, which is a waste of the organization's time and money.

So they will expect serious applicants to have taken the trouble to find out something about the job before applying for it. This would be the sensible thing to do anyway, but it is surprising how many applicants turn up for interviews with precious little idea of what the organization or job are like.

You *should* already have a general impression of what the job involves and what the function of the employing organization is when you make your initial application, but if you are given an interview it is worth doing a little more to further this knowledge. The sources of such information vary according to the job in question, but careers masters, college appointments boards, careers officers, friends and relatives may all be able to tell you something about the organization and what they do. Quite possibly they will refer you to publications such as *The job book: training and career choices for school and college leavers* (Hobsons Press), which is readily available in libraries. On top of all this, many employers send out fairly detailed descriptions of both the job and the company as a whole with the application forms. Where they do this, careful reading of the material sent is frequently sufficient in itself. If the organization concerned is situated not very far from you, then perhaps you might kill two birds with one stone by going round there to get any literature that may be available (such as the company's last annual report, which may also be obtained from the Company Secretary). Apart from the background information you may obtain, a visit to the place where the interview will be held will familiarize you with it and help you get the 'feel' of the place in advance, and may give you greater confidence. Thus you can reassure the potential employer of your serious interest in the job and of your sensible approach to things by making sure that you know a reasonable amount about the job and its context. You can also help yourself a lot by finding out about the selection procedures used by the different organizations. If you have an interview with the representatives of a company and know that one of your friends has already been seen by the same company, ask him or her about the interview, the kind of questions asked, whether or not any tests were given and so on. Then you will know roughly what to expect. If you and your friend are in direct competition for the same job, you may of course meet with an unsympathetic response to your questions!

REVIEWING AND PREPARING THE MAIN TOPIC AREAS

It is important to think about the interview in advance and to review the sort of information you may be asked for. From the last chapter you will have gathered that much of the interview is spent looking backwards at what you have done in the past, and why you have done it. If suddenly confronted with questions of this kind, the normal response of the applicant is to provide an answer as quickly as possible. Yet looking back over a period of some years may not be that easy and answers given on the spur of the moment in an interview may not be accurate; given time to think about questions of this sort, the applicant might give a very different answer (as some of them realize afterwards, prompting the reaction, 'Why on earth did I say that?') It is best to think over these sort of questions in advance as far as that is possible. And it *is* possible: with a degree of intelligent anticipation, you can spot the sort of questions that are likely to arise. Some clue is often given by the application form; if it asks for information about family background (e.g. parents' occupations) then this may be seen as being of some relevance and will quite possibly be followed up with questions in the interview. Likewise, if the form asks you to list interests, the interviewer will probably pick up on this and ask questions about those leisure pursuits you have listed. It was suggested in Chapter 2 that you should photocopy the application form after completing it; if you did this, you should refer to the form prior to the interview. Apart from the clues you might get from the application form, and anything you hear from other people you know who have been interviewed by the same organization, you have the guidance given here which (with a little intelligent application on your part) should also assist in forming some expectations of the type of things you are likely to be asked.

In order to structure your preparation and thinking about interviews, an Interview Preparation Programme and Checklist is provided in the Appendix, p. 90. This shows, in detail, the sort of questions interviewers ask and covers most of the topics that they are likely to introduce. If you now turn to it briefly you will see how it is laid out and what it consists of. This structured guide to self-review should be gone through slowly, as the instructions tell you, after you have read the rest of this book. For the moment, all we need to do here is make some general points about preparing for questions under each of the main topic areas discussed previously. The emphasis should be on identifying the sort of information *you* wish to get across in the interview as well as on coping adequately with the interviewer's questions.

Family background

These questions are fairly straightforward, predictable and easy to answer. Sometimes applicants are reluctant to let an interviewer know that they have come from a relatively disadvantaged background, but as was pointed out on p. 35, this information can work to their credit if the interviewer is trying to assess how well they have done in light of the opportunities open to them. So do *not* be shy about putting across facts that are going to work in your favour; if you have had a steep hill to climb to get where you are now, let it be known. Your circumstances in the past often lead on to consideration of your circumstances at present. This is where female applicants face the potentially hazardous questions of marital and family aspirations. Interviewers may justify asking questions about whether a woman is married and whether she intends having children as simply trying to get a fuller picture of her as a person. But, notwithstanding equal opportunities legislation, one suspects some of them will treat the information that a woman intends giving up work (even temporarily) to have a family as being a reason for not employing them. In a situation of this kind, perhaps the applicant is within her rights if she says something along the lines of 'I really have not thought seriously about that [having children] yet, so I could not say', or 'I am not sure whether I will or not', or just 'No, I do not want to have any children – at least, that's the way I feel about it now.' When thinking about this, it is worth remembering that the use of such information in making selection decisions is a breach of the law in most cases anyway.

Education and training

Again, these questions are, on the whole, easy to cope with providing you have given them a little thought beforehand. A poor record in examinations can be a little tricky if it is mentioned. Interviewers sometimes ask if there is any special reason for doing badly in some or all of the examinations; if there is, by all means give it. Unfortunately, if you make too much of it, there is a danger that it will be dismissed as 'just making excuses'. So do not play too heavily on your excuses, no matter how genuine they are; it might be better, for example, to mention the extenuating circumstances but admit that you do not know just how much difference they have made to the final results (though the implication may be 'a lot').

Generally, an ability to form and express opinions in your education and training is one of the things the interviewer will look for. Typical questions are given in the Appendix; the important thing to note here is that an endless recital of criticisms is in itself unlikely to win you any applause; you should try to be constructive in your views. So if you have a criticism of the way a course is run or of the type of institution you are attending, be prepared not only to make that point but also to suggest how you feel things could be improved.

Work experience

If you have any work experience, the aspects of it to think about in advance of the interview are the reasons you had for joining and leaving the organizations you have worked for, what you did in those jobs which you can point to as relevant and useful to the job you are applying for now, what you were especially successful at, how you dealt with the problems and how you got on with colleagues. All these entail refreshing your memory and thinking over, otherwise your answers may seem vague and hesitant and generally lacking in conviction. If a candidate seems uncertain and vague about the reasons for taking and leaving the jobs he has had, the impression will be that he has drifted aimlessly through them. Particular care must be taken in considering what you will say (and how it will be interpreted) concerning your reasons for wanting to leave your present job and join *this* organization.

Motivation and aspirations

There are very few direct questions on this; as we saw earlier most of what the interviewer knows of the candidate's motivation and aspirations is inferred from what the candidate says over the course of the interview. If you do have an idea of what you want to do now and in the near future, you will come across as being a person who knows where he is going, which will probably be to the good. The value of knowing something about the job and the company comes when the interviewer asks why you want this job and what specifically attracts you to it; your level of motivation will not impress if you have not got the faintest idea of what it is all about. However, there is no need to imply that this is absolutely the only kind of job you have considered.

Looking further ahead in time, the interviewer might ask 'How do you see your career developing over,

say, the next five years?'; it is as well to have given some
thought to how you would like things to go, providing
this is coloured by reality - but obviously any such
aspirations should not be inflexible. People and
circumstances change over time, so any ideas you have
now on how you want your career to develop should
not be too fixed. The interviewer is unlikely to be much
more impressed by someone with a very rigid set of
aims for the future than by someone who as yet has no
aims at all. Another aspect of this is the degree of
ambition you show. A dim view is likely to be taken of
anyone who is devoid of ambition, but the same
sometimes goes for a candidate who has a very high
level of ambition; the excessively ambitious may be
hard to satisfy and leave the company after a year or
two, before the investment put into him in the form of
recruitment and training provides any return.

One type of question that does not fit well under any
of the normal headings, but which might be loosely
related to motivation, is the one which invites you to
assess your own strengths and weaknesses (in general and
in relation to the job) in a very direct fashion. In other
words, questions which require you to 'sell' yourself.
Sometimes they are delivered with all the subtlety of a
sledge-hammer - 'What makes you think you would do
this job well?' A more lethal form of this can come
before the interview, when a candidate may be asked to
write a description of himself first as if written by a
friend and then as if written by a critic. We will have
more to say on the handling of questions like this later,
but for the moment you should think about them for
yourself. What experience, training, qualifications and
personal qualities are there in your favour relevant to
the job? What are your strengths overall? What
weaknesses are there in your abilities, experience, etc.,
and what would the interviewer's reaction be to them?
If you did not admit to any weaknesses, e.g. being bad at
figure-work, would he believe you? Would you believe
anyone who said that? Questions of this kind are
difficult and need a lot of thought in advance.

Finally, one direct question that often comes up and may be taken as an indication of your motivation is 'Are you willing to move to another part of the country if the company wants you to?' Mobility may be a vital requirement of the job, so you had better decide beforehand whether you are willing to be moved around the country. Do not dismiss the idea too quickly, as moving around can help you develop as an individual, quite apart from increasing your employment prospects.

Leisure interests

These should be fairly easy for you to talk about. One of the main dangers is 'freezing' in the interview when asked things like 'I see you like reading. What was the last book you read?' Normally such questions would be simple, but many an interviewee will testify to the wonderful ease with which the mind goes blank at moments like this, with the result that the interviewer begins to doubt whether you really do any reading at all. A little thought in advance about the likely questions should reduce the chances of this kind of mental paralysis gripping you.

Two of the points that frequently arise are just how much time you have to spend on a pursuit for it to be an interest, and whether one should only mention interests that are likely to impress interviewers. Taking the first point, there is no simple answer to this and it remains a matter of judgement. Resist the temptation to give almost everything you ever do as an interest. For instance, if you claim that you are interested in the theatre and it is discovered that you have been only once in the last year, you are going to look a trifle foolish (barring extenuating circumstances, such as long distance, finance, etc.). If you are going to give a particular activity as one of your leisure pursuits it should be something that you do fairly regularly and which you feel you can talk about if asked. You should go for depth of interest rather than a large range of shallow interests.

Turning to the second point, by all means emphasize the more socially impressive interests to an interviewer if you have a range of things to which you devote more or less equal amounts of time. But do not try to paint a false picture of your leisure activities in the hope of making yourself look good. When contestants in beauty queen contests are chatted to by the compère, they are often asked what they do in their spare time. All too often they produce a carefully balanced list, like reading, water-skiing, sub-aqua diving and embroidery. To find so many attractive girls with the same neat blend of the intellectual, the athletic and the female in their interests is so unlikely that they lack credibility. The beauty queens have other merits that make such minor considerations fade into the background, but, alas, this is not the case for interviewees. If they depart far from the truth in this respect, the interviewers are quite likely to find out. If you do not really know anything about what you profess to be one of your interests, you may be discredited in every other way too. Another aspect of this is that some candidates feel that the things they do in their time off are somehow not 'respectable' enough to give as interests. These include activities such as watching television, listening to rock and roll music and going out with friends to parties, pubs, etc. In fact, most interviewers would be surprised if candidates (particularly young ones) did not spend some of their time doing these things. They may not be 'formal' interests such as chess, football, photography, literature and so on, but they are certainly better to mention than nothing at all. And if you do have *no* interests at all due to some particular personal circumstances, make sure the interviewer realizes that there are reasons for this lack of activity.

Finally, if there are any indications that you are particularly good at one of your hobbies (e.g. representing your college in it), or if you take some part, no matter how modest, in organizing leisure activities for others (secretary of a society, for instance), try to ensure that this information is conveyed in the

interview if the chance arises: make it one of your
objectives to get this across in the interview.

General topics

There are four main sources of these topics: things in
the news at the time, things related to the job or the
organization, things the applicant says in the course of
the interview or on the application form and (worst of
all) anything that happens to interest the interviewer.

How can you prepare for these? Well there is not a
great deal you can do, which is precisely the point (or
one of them) of asking questions on current affairs,
social issues and so forth - you have to 'think on your
feet' in dealing with the questions. One useful step is to
read the newspapers and watch news and current affairs
programmes on TV thoroughly during the period you
are applying for jobs (even if you do not do so
normally); then you will at least be familiar with what
is going on and can spot anything that looks
particularly relevant to this job or to this organization
and its operations. If you have also formed views of
your own on the main issues, all the better. Remember
here that the interviewers are unlikely to ask questions
on overtly political or religious matters, so that cuts
down the field somewhat. However, the range of
possible topics is still formidable. Fortunately, there is
a tendency to concentrate on the 'big' issues; just one
example would be energy policy and the pros and cons
of investing in a large-scale nuclear power programme;
try thinking of some others yourself.

As far as topics arising out of the candidate's
comments or application form are concerned, these
will probably relate to things that he or she knows
something about and has views on anyway. Wider
issues relating to the organization's functions or
products are topics that can be anticipated to some
extent.

The real problem comes from the other source of
such topics, namely the interviewer's own particular
interests. It is quite unfair for interviewers to expect

candidates to be able to talk about anything they choose to light upon, but they sometimes seem to expect precisely that. If this happens, the candidate can try to bluff his way through or admit that this just happens to be a topic he or she knows little or nothing about; the latter course is the better bet.

Specialist and technical matters

Potentially, anything relating to your specialist field could be asked. Fortunately, however, some narrowing down of this wide range can again be achieved by prior consideration. Questions in this area are most often focused on any project work the candidate has done (or on any other indication of his specialised interest within his discipline), or on the application of his training to particular facets of the job he is applying for. In thinking over these themes when preparing for an interview, it is as well to keep in mind that the interviewers are not always specialists, or specialists of the same kind as the candidate - in effect, they are laymen. It is thus wise to think in terms of having to communicate technical information in a way that anyone can understand. Some specialists who carry out interviews do ask questions of a technical nature over a wide area of the subject concerned. Clearly, you cannot revise everything just for an interview, but it might be wise to brush-up on your weakest points.

Health

No preparation needed. If you have indicated some physical handicap or history of illness on the application form and this is taken up in the interview, you will no doubt be all too well aware of it to need any consideration beforehand.

THE UNPREDICTABLE ELEMENTS

In case you have now slipped into the cosy notion that interviews, given sensible preparation, are entirely predictable, it is important that you be dragged back to reality. *No* interview is 100% predictable or anything like it. There are always surprises, things you did not expect, even if it follows the kind of planned approach in exactly the same way as described here. This should not frighten you though (after all, what worthwhile and interesting conversation between two people ever runs *exactly* according to expectations - if it did, it would be rather dull). Looking at an interview in a positive light, as a potentially interesting and stimulating experience, you should welcome a reasonable degree of unpredictability, as a challenge. What one wants to avoid is an interview in which, through the interviewee being quite unprepared, *every* question comes as something unexpected. The result of the latter is that the interviewee may never really get comfortable in responding to the straightforward questions, let alone achieving the state of mind where he is ready to respond to the more challenging ones.

REHEARSAL: THE BEST LAID PLANS . . .

Another warning note should be sounded here. All the guidance given on preparing for interviews, including the Interview Preparation Programme and Checklist, are intended to direct your memory and thought to the areas and types of questioning you are most likely to encounter; they are *not* there to help you to form precise answers that can be recited in the interview. Rehearsing word-perfect answers is not a good idea at all. We have just talked about the unpredictable elements of interviews, and one aspect of this is that questions you may be expecting seldom come out in *precisely* the way you anticipated. You might, for example, be expecting the question 'What are your leisure interests?', but the actual question asked is 'What do you get out of your leisure interests?' Too often, a candidate will hear the words 'leisure interests' and they will trigger off his carefully prepared response which may well neglect the real nature of the question. So in this example, he might start by replying along the lines of 'Well, I play a lot of sport; I enjoy football particularly, and I suppose I do quite a lot of reading . . .' This is not a reply to the question asked, it is a reply to the question anticipated. If the candidate persists in doing this (not quite answering the question as posed) the interviewer may well become somewhat irritated, or may conclude that the candidate, for some reason best known to himself, is being deliberately evasive.

Apart from this tendency to give prepared answers irrespective of the wording of the question, there is the other danger that precisely formulated answers have a nasty habit of not coming out quite as they were meant to in the interview. So perhaps the only time one would be advised to really think out the wording of a reply in detail beforehand would be where specialist or technical questions are likely to be asked. For example, if you have done a thesis or project, you will very often be asked about it. The interviewer, if he is a specialist in the same general areas as you, may still not be all that familiar with this particular topic, so if you are describing the project work to him, it is important that you can put it across clearly and concisely; you should explain it in such a way that a person who is not as familiar with the field as you are can grasp the essence of it. If you have reason for believing that the interviewers (or some of them) may be non-specialists or administrators, then it is even more important that you can convey what you have done in a non-technical way. To do this, and to do it in such a way that it can be communicated in a very limited amount of time, requires considerable thought in advance of the interview. In this instance, some actual rehearsal of a pre-planned answer may well pay dividends.

PREPARING YOUR OWN QUESTIONS

Questioning in interviews is seldom an entirely one-way process. You will usually be given a chance to put questions of your own at the end of the interview. This is not meant for you to ask, as I heard one applicant ask, 'Where can I get a No. 37 bus?' It is your opportunity to fill in the gaps in your information about the job, working conditions, promotion prospects, etc. Quite apart from the value of finding answers to your questions, it is probably in your interests to have some questions to ask, if only for the sake of appearances. Interviewers will be more inclined to judge a candidate's intentions as being 'serious' if he shows a lively interest in the job and future prospects. Again, the best strategy is to get clear in your mind the questions you want to ask before you go to the interview, otherwise you are likely to find, as many have before you, that at the end of an (often searching) interview you are mentally fatigued and your mind goes blank when you are offered the chance to ask questions.

Incidentally, do not make the questions too numerous or too detailed; the interviewer, in large organizations anyway, cannot know all the details of all the jobs that may eventually be open to you. Also, he has limited time, so you must gauge the extent to which he is willing to go on answering questions.

ADOPTING THE RIGHT ATTITUDE

If you do not get very worked-up over attending interviews, then you have little problem in this respect. You can of course be over-confident and not take things as seriously as they should be. I remember having an interview for a job that I was not sure whether or not I wanted. I found myself getting quite tense waiting outside the interview room and so I thought 'This is ridiculous – getting worked up over a job that I'm not sure I want'. I started thinking about the negative aspects of the job, and when I was called in a few minutes later, I had thought myself into the mood where I did not care very much whether the job was offered or not. This relatively detached attitude was of itself no bad thing, but no sooner had the four-man selection board introduced themselves in a very

business-like and efficient manner than there was a
loud 'thud'. All eyes turned toward the windows from
whence this noise came, and outside we saw the top of a
ladder, from which rapidly sprouted a window-cleaner
clutching a bucket and sponge. He proceeded to noisily
clean the windows while the interview was in progress.
The consternation and embarrassment this caused the
board, along with the sheer silliness of the situation
which appealed to my sense of humour, combined to
make me wildly over-confident. I found it difficult to
take the proceedings seriously and started cracking
jokes. Needless to say, I did not get the job! I ascertained
afterwards that my attitude in the interview was the
main thing that went against me.

I mention this anecdote simply to show that one can
be *too* relaxed and confident in an interview. To be just
a little anxious, a little keyed-up about interviews is
good: it generally facilitates performance rather than
inhibits it. Only when you become very anxious do you
begin to harm your prospects. Some advice on how to
'keep your cool' in this kind of situation will be given
in later sections of this chapter and the next, but, if you
tend to get over anxious about interviews, your first
concern should be your overall attitude towards them.
One of the problems here is that some candidates see
interviews as basically threatening situations; they
worry about their own deficiencies, about how nervous
they get, about what the interviewers will think of
them, about failing to get the job, and so on. It is as if
the 'fear of failure' overcomes their 'need for achievement'. Stressing the negative aspects of the procedure
like this does little good. If you can, try to reconstrue
the interview in a more positive light. This, admittedly,
is easy to say but not so easy to do. However, the
following lines of thought have proved helpful to
others and may also be useful to you in this respect.

If you can arouse some curiosity in the procedure it
can help make it a more pleasant experience. What sort
of things will they ask, what sort of approach will they
take, what sort of person are they after? Treat it like a

guessing game, a battle of wits: can you anticipate the interviewers and prepare accordingly? This outlook makes the interview more of an interesting and challenging experience. And the more interested you are, the more that interest will convey itself in the interview itself, which will do you no harm at all.

Alternatively, you may prefer to look on the interview as a joint problem-solving exercise between you and the interviewer in which you will cooperate together to find whether this is really the job for you, whether you would be able to do it well, and whether you would be happy doing it.

Another strategy is to go in to the interview with low expectations, saying to yourself 'I probably have not got a chance of this job, but I will do as well as I can in the interview because it will be good practice for other occasions'. Mentally writing-off your chances in this way obviously has its dangers (as has the similar approach of trying to persuade yourself that this job probably is not all that good anyway) but it can sometimes create a more relaxed and detached approach that can be helpful to some people. Others may be happier if they can look on the bright side and keep in mind that of all the people to apply for this job, they are amongst the very few selected for interview, so they must be suitable on paper at very least. These different ways of thinking about the interview all have their advantages and disadvantages. Whether or not you use any of them is for you to decide; choose whichever you feel most comfortable with and easiest to sustain.

If they give you a more positive outlook and reduce your anxiety level even partially, they will be of some value in improving your attitude to the interview.

PERSONAL APPEARANCE AND DRESS

While there is no doubt that views on what is and what is not acceptable in terms of personal appearance and dress have relaxed considerably over recent years, you should not be lulled into thinking that this is no longer important. Most interviewers are willing to accept (in some cases, perhaps it is more a case of 'resigned to') candidates with long hair, flamboyant styles and colours of clothing and so on, *providing* they are neat, clean and smart in appearance. So while it is not necessary (unless you want to play really safe) to have a short back and sides haircut and to don the most conservative suit you can lay hands on, it is wise to take some care over your appearance and to turn up in something a bit more impressive than denim.

For candidates of either sex, it is important that they show they have taken some care over their appearance for the interview; after all, if they cannot be bothered about how they look on this occasion, the interviewer will have just cause for doubting whether they will when they are working either, which may be important in some jobs where the individual will be representing the organization. The other thing here, of course, is that an interviewer may, rightly or wrongly, infer something about how serious a candidate's interest in a job is from how much attention he or she has paid to personal appearance. So remember to make sure that your hair, finger nails, shoes and clothes are all clean; it is surprising how many people neglect one or other of these.

One sometimes hears the view expressed that an applicant should dress as he likes and not put on any special effort for the benefit of an interview, because if it is the kind of organization that cares so much about such superficial things as how someone looks, then it probably is not worth working for anyway. Applicants who say this are in effect selecting themselves *out* of companies whose values they think they probably do not share. Well, fine - that is their right if they so wish. One of the problems with this strategy, however, is that interviewers are not always truly representative of the climate and values of the organizations they are recruiting for. So a candidate may be rejected because of his appearance simply on the basis of the interviewer's prejudices, while if he had been taken in to that organization he might have found a far more relaxed and congenial atmosphere that suited him perfectly.

It is certainly true that one can no more tell which is the best candidate by his or her appearance than one can judge a book by its cover. Judging by appearances is apt to be misleading. Nonetheless, first impressions are very powerful, and the interviewer's first impressions of an applicant are strongly coloured by the personal appearance of the latter. And in some cases there *is* a good reason for assessing people on their appearance, as in the case of jobs where the individual will have a high degree of public contact, and should thus be very 'presentable'. Even if the job in question is not of this kind, there is often the possibility that later transfers or promotions will put an individual in a position which does have representative duties.

Finally, apart from dressing in clothes that will look good, try to make sure that you *feel* good in them too. Avoid things which are too heavy or thick, or too tight or anything else that is likely to make you feel uncomfortable (e.g. some people find nylon shirts tend to make them perspire when they are tense) in the interview. Ideally, you want to dress in clothes that are not only neat and smart, but in which you feel *relaxed* and comfortable as well.

IMMEDIATELY BEFORE THE INTERVIEW

There are a few sensible steps you can take just before the interview which can help you, not least in respect of your state of mind when you arrive.

Travelling. It may sound like a statement of the obvious, but you need to work out precisely where you are going, and how to get there, well in advance. A surprising number of candidates manage to turn up late because they have not done this. You must leave yourself an adequate safety margin in timing your journey to take account of the vagaries of public transport, traffic jams, etc. Delays on the journey, even if they do not actually make you late, can cause anxiety if you have not left yourself adequate time. You can do without worries of this kind, so do not cut things too fine. A more leisurely-paced journey will leave you in a better mental state.

Relaxation. Comments relating to this have already been made in connection with the clothes you wear, your travel arrangements and your general attitude. There is no one single trick that will ensure a relaxed feeling in the interview. There are special deep-relaxation techniques but these are time-consuming and need expert supervision. If you are the sort of individual who gets very nervous waiting for an interview, you might try the following technique: close your eyes, breathe in and out *evenly, slowly* and *deeply* and say (to yourself) 'One' each time you breathe out. Concentrate on your breathing, and gradually relax your body as much as possible; focus your attention on different groups of muscles in succession (e.g. back of the neck and shoulders, stomach, legs) until you are as relaxed as you can get. This kind of relaxation technique used before an interview sometimes helps produce a more calm yet alert state of mind, particularly if it has been practised on a number of occasions.

One type of relaxing agent *not* recommended is alcohol. It may make you feel better to have a couple of drinks before an interview, but the anaesthetic effect will probably impair your concentration, and anyway interviewers are not notorious for the generosity of their assessments when they detect the smell of beer or spirits wafting across from the candidate (sucking mints is a woefully inadequate remedy).

You can help yourself a great deal, not just in relaxing but in terms of your whole state of mind, by ensuring you get a good night's sleep the night before the interview. So try to arrange things in such a way that you give yourself the chance to have a good night's rest; avoid anything that will keep you up very late and leave you feeling tired and left-over the next day. And talking of basic needs or functions, do not forget the wonderfully laxative quality interviews sometimes have! Go to the toilet before you set out on your journey, and leave yourself enough time to go again (if needs be) before entering the interview room. One other point about keeping calm before the interview. Should you have left a safety margin in the timing of your journey and arrived a little early, you can kill time by having a look around the area or by simply sitting in the waiting room. Either way, it is often a good idea to take something to read – the more engrossing the better!

SUMMARY OF ADVICE

Pulling together the advice given on preparing for an interview, you should:

(a) Get all the practice you can at 'being interviewed'.

(b) Find out something about the organization which is interviewing you, about its products or services, and about the job itself. If you can also discover what sort of selection procedures they use, or the kind of things asked in the interview (from other people who have been through it), so much the better.

(c) Review and prepare the main topic areas, using the Interview Preparation Programme and Checklist. Use this to think ahead, to anticipate the kind of questions you might encounter. What general lines will your answers take, and what sort of picture will this convey to the interviewer (bearing in mind the ways in which he might use the information, as outlined on pp. 34-44)? Is it the picture you would like to project, and (or?) is it accurate in so far as you can be objective about it?

(d) Prepare any answers you are likely to give about a thesis or other piece of specialist work with particular care. They need to be concise and clear, so that interviewers not involved in your field will still be able to understand and appreciate what you have done.

(e) If interviews, or the thought of them, makes you over anxious, try to change your perceptions of them in line with the kind of alternatives suggested here. If you get to think about them differently, you may find that you begin to react differently too.

(f) Put on as clean, tidy and well-dressed (conservative if in doubt) appearance as you can manage for the interview.

(g) Make sure that you know how to get there properly and that you leave sufficient safety margin in timing your journey (and take the letter giving you the time and date of the interview with you).

6

Putting Yourself Across in the Interview

RECEPTION, AND THE IMPORTANCE OF FIRST IMPRESSIONS

We saw earlier (p. 22) that interviewers sometimes make up their minds about candidates too early on in the interview, and we know from our everyday lives that first impressions can have a powerful and long-lasting effect. When we have a set or expectancy to see people a particular way, we go on seeing them that way because we tend to ignore information that contradicts our viewpoint or we reinterpret the new information so that it is made to fit in with our existing perceptions. The early part of the interview is thus very important, all the more so with interviews being so short anyway; if you get off on the wrong foot there is not a lot of time to put things right. Fortunately, some interviewers make allowances for nerves etc. at the start of an interview, but you cannot count on that. So let us look at how you tackle the introduction.

INTRODUCTIONS

First things first; when you enter the interview room, do not forget to close the door behind you. As you face the interviewer(s), try to raise a quiet smile and walk over to the chair ready for you, but do not sit down until invited to do so. The way interviewers greet you varies enormously; they are often not sure themselves how best to do it so that it puts you at ease. Some go the whole hog and stand up, shake you by the hand and introduce themselves and (if it is a board interview) their colleagues. Others simply stay seated and issue a perfunctory greeting. You just have to play this as it comes, but do not offer to shake hands unless the interviewer proffers his. If it is difficult for you to remember names first time round - and in board interviews it is even more difficult - make a conscious effort to do so at this point; it helps if you can quickly use the name after you are introduced by saying 'Good Morning Mr Smith' or 'How do you do, Mrs Davies', or whatever.

Irrespective of the kind of greeting you get, *look the interviewer in the eye*. Likewise with board interviews, do not just look at the Chairman, give the others a brief glance and smile too (maybe even a nod!). You do not have to keep this smile plastered grimly to your face as it is really only a good thing to do when you come in, are introduced, at appropriate lighter moments in the interview and when you say goodbye.

To sum up the introduction. Take your lead from the interviewer, look at him, put on a reasonably pleasant face and try to appear as if you are glad to be there even if you feel as though you are facing a firing squad.

COMBATING INTERVIEW NERVES

This was looked at in terms of preparation in the previous chapter. The better your preparation, the more confident you are likely to be. However, all but a few people will still feel a little tense in interviews. In fact, if it is any compensation, even some of the interviewers do too. What can you do to keep calm when you are actually in there? Firstly, try to sit comfortably without actually slouching. Do *not* smoke unless you are invited to do so (if you *desperately* need a cigarette, you might risk asking if it is all right). And do not chew gum or anything else either, as I have seen one or two people do! Take your time over your answers to questions; a common mistake is to blurt out the first thing that comes into one's head, which soon makes things seem worse. Give yourself a second or two before answering, and consciously check yourself if you are talking much faster than normal. You can, of course, be too slow and deliberate in answering, but few people go this far and rushing your answers is a much greater danger.

Sometimes an interviewer or members of a panel may, perhaps because of their manner or because someone is silly enough to try deliberately to put stress on you, seem rather threatening and hostile; obviously, this is very off-putting. If you encounter this kind of situation and experience a lot of anxiety, you might find a technique used by allied prisoners-of-war on their guards of some value. If a guard was being particularly threatening – say, shouting angrily in the prisoner's face – the POW would try to imagine him exactly as he was, standing there in front of him and shouting his head off, but stark naked. It is wonderful how much dignity and authority depart with one's clothing – the POWs certainly found that imagining the guards naked made them much less threatening figures. And providing you have just a little imagination, it can work extremely well with bombastic or arrogant interviewers too. All you have to do is to imagine them, sitting there behind their desk with all their papers in front of them – but stark naked! If your imagination is vivid, I should warn you that this technique can be dangerous and has been known to lead to interviewees smirking or giggling for no apparent reason in front of perplexed interviewers. A variation on the theme is to imagine the interview as a toothbrush, or something equally ludicrous. Try it out on someone else in another situation and see if it works for you.

TACTICS IN DEALING WITH DIFFERENT TYPES OF QUESTION

There are a number of different types of question you will meet in an interview, and the main ones are listed below along with some hints on dealing with them. Putting this into practice may be difficult first time round, but you will grow more adept with each interview.

Closed questions. These are the ones we talked about earlier (p. 23) which require only 'yes' or 'no', or similarly brief answers. Nothing difficult about that for you. But you may find that some inexperienced, or just ineffective, interviewers ask so many questions of this type that you do not get a chance to say very much. This is the only way closed questions cause problems, by stopping you from putting across information you feel might help your chances of getting the job. In those circumstances, you have to take the initiative by giving more information than is strictly called for by the question. This is discussed further below, in the section on helping less competent interviewers.

Open questions. This is where the interviewer gives you the chance to talk, by asking questions like 'What do you like doing in your spare time?', or 'Tell me something about your time at college.' All well and good: you can use the opportunity to put over the things you want to communicate about yourself. If you have prepared properly, you will know what you want to get across and will concentrate on that. If you have not bothered to prepare and have not thought about the likely questions, then open-ended ones can be a problem: they give you so much scope for answering that you sometimes do not know where to begin, what to put in and what to leave out.

Hypothetical questions. No, this does not mean questions you might be asked. It is the name given to

questions of the 'What would you do *if* . . . ?' variety.
Questions which put you in an imaginary situation
and ask you how you would deal with it: for example,
'Say you were in charge of some staff who were older
than yourself and who resented having a younger
supervisor, how would you deal with them?' These
questions are of very dubious value, mainly because
what a person says he would do in no way guarantees
that he would act that way if really faced with the
situation. Also, the situation is only sketchily outlined,
and that is what you must emphasize in your answer; in
real life you would know *much* more about the people
and/or the situation concerned, and this knowledge
would almost certainly influence the way in which you
tackled the matter. Having made that point tactfully,
you can go on to answer the question as best you can. If
the interviewer does not like the particular line of
thought you give in answer to this hypothetical
question, at least he has been made aware of the fact
that a truly accurate answer is impossible. Another
answer that is sometimes appropriate, particularly if
the interviewer asks you to say how you would sort out
a particular kind of problem, is to preface your reply
with a statement to the effect that you would hope you
could avoid that kind of problem arising anyway (if, of
course, it seems avoidable to you). You might then say
'But if it did, then I would . . .'.

Multiple questions. Even the most experienced and
well-trained interviewers succumb to the error of
asking multiple questions now and then. As the term
implies, these are questions delivered in a string - you
get not one question, but several at once. For example:

'What sort of things do you like doing in your time
off?
Do you read much? or go to the cinema - have you
seen this latest film that everyone is talking about?'

Sometimes half a dozen questions cascade out like this
in a single sentence. The interviewer starts with one

idea, but as he asks the question, he changes his mind either about what precisely he wants to know or how to put it. The result is something of a mess, the interviewee not knowing quite which question he is supposed to answer, or whether to answer all of them. Very often, the first question asked is the best one - the interviewer should bite his lip if he feels the need to elaborate on it. You could answer the first one and help him, or answer the very last one which usually gives the least information; if you do not really want to talk about the topic much, answer the question that gives the least scope. Multiple questions, if you think fast enough, give you the chance to try to limit or expand how much you say on a topic by choosing which element(s) of them to answer. The greatest danger is that of becoming confused and trying to answer all of the questions at once; in this case, your answer becomes as ill-thought-out as the question.

Leading questions have been discussed on p. 41. The interviewer indicates the kind of answer he expects when he asks a leading question, e.g. 'You will have to move around a lot in this job; does that appeal to you?' Most people, when presented with a question like that not unnaturally tell the interviewer what he expects or wants to hear. If you feel especially truthful and do not want to give the answer he expects, then you could go ahead and surprise him; at least he might give you credit for your independence. Generally speaking, though, it is best not to rock the boat: go where leading questions lead you, unless you feel it very important not to.

Unexpected or difficult questions obviously take many shapes and forms, but one of the common needs interviewees have in the face of them is time to think out an answer. Firstly, you should, of course, give yourself a moment to think rather than trying to start your reply immediately, whether or not you have any idea of what you are really saying. On the other hand, you can only take a second or two before starting to reply – much longer than that and you may appear a bit dim. This does not allow much time for thought, so is there any way you can buy more time? One useful little device is to say something along the lines of 'How exactly do you mean?' – a tactic that makes the interviewer rephrase his question so as to make himself clearer, thus allowing you more time to sort out your answer. However, you must use this technique very sparingly, not more than twice in any one interview, and only for the most difficult sorts of question (otherwise you will simply be thought a bit dim for not understanding the first time round).

Some questions asked in interviews are not just difficult, they are almost impossible to answer. One interviewer I heard asked a candidate how he thought we could cure inflation, to which the candidate reasonably replied that since the Government had failed to do so, he did not think he had much chance of coming up with a solution to it either. Questions which go beyond what you can reasonably hope to answer in the limited time of an interview, or which defy any clear answer anyway, should be gently and diplomatically pointed out as such to the interviewer in the course of attempting to answer them.

One tactic you should *not* try is being evasive. Dealing with a difficult question by answering one slightly different from that asked might work just once, but doing it persistently simply irritates interviewers and will work against you.

THE SOUND OF SILENCE

A few seconds of silence in an interview seems like an eternity, both to interviewers and to candidates. The important thing is not to be panicked by it. As has been pointed out already, it is better to take a second or two to think out an answer if need be rather than to launch into an answer prematurely. Silences are a problem for the interviewer as well. Sometimes they come about because the interviewer has forgotten what he was going to ask or simply cannot think of anything else to ask, which usually causes him some discomfort. And silence on the part of an interviewee following a question leaves him with a difficult decision to make: does he assume that the interviewee is just thinking out his answer or that he is completely nonplussed by the question and in need of rescue? The interviewer has to know when a pregnant pause becomes an embarrassed silence.

Some interviewers do actually use silence to put pressure on you. They ask a question, and then remain silent when you have finished answering. This unsettles a lot of candidates, and, assuming that more is required, they start desperately trying to elaborate on what has generally been a perfectly adequate answer. Do not fall into this nasty little trap: if the interviewer remains silent when you have finished answering, you remain silent too, even if it is difficult to do so. If the interviewer wants you to elaborate further, or seeks clarification of what you have already said, let him ask for it.

ASSERTIVE BEHAVIOUR

The central theme of this book is that you do not have to be totally passive in an interview; for example, you can do a lot to help your chances by actively trying to get across the information you want to communicate. In other words, you must assert yourself to a degree. Some of the main aspects of this assertive behaviour are dealt with in this section.

Your attitude

Just how assertive should one be? Are you expected to 'sell' yourself directly and unambiguously in an interview? Usually not, though there are some interviewers who invite you to do so by asking questions like 'What have you got to offer us, Miss X?', or 'Now, tell me why you think you will do a good job for us?' Where this happens, you know where you stand and can quite shamelessly start 'selling'. However, most interviewers, and candidates, do draw back from anything quite as blunt as this approach. What candidates must usually do, it seems, is to project a modest, slightly submissive image, while somehow making sure that their good points are noted. The latter often has to be achieved by the interviewee subtly drawing attention to his good points in the course of answering questions, making sure that they do come out in the interview irrespective of whether the interviewer asks the right questions or not. But this must be done gently, unobtrusively and without any hint of bragging or overtly trying to control the interview.

Apart from this, there are two other aspects of one's attitude in an interview that we should talk about. Firstly, *enthusiasm*. This is vital. You must look and sound as though you are interested and keen both about the job and even about the interview itself. You know the difference there is in your face and voice when talking about something that really interests you and which you like, as compared to when you are talking of something which you dislike and find boring. You must aim for the former in an interview. Lack of interest or enthusiasm will convey itself to the interviewer very quickly, and will probably be taken as a lack of commitment on your part, with gloomy results.

The second point concerns humour. Is one supposed to be very serious at interviews? Being fairly serious and earnest will probably not go against you, providing you do not keep a stony face when the interviewer cracks a joke. But some sign of a sense of humour can work very much in your favour. No one can tell you how to go about this, of course, as it obviously depends on the opportunity given. Forced humour out of context will not be received very favourably, and nor will excessive flippancy. So it is a question of your own judgement as to whether or not you inject an occasional flash of wit into the proceedings; if done in the appropriate way, it works very well.

Talking

If an interview is being conducted well, you should not
really need to assert yourself in terms of the amount of
talking you do as you will be doing most of it anyway.
If it is conducted badly, with a lot of closed questions,
this gives you less scope to talk, as we noted earlier –
and the advice given earlier (p. 71) holds. What we
should look at here are other aspects of asserting
yourself when talking. A very basic one is speaking up;
an amazing number of candidates (probably through
anxiety) speak so quietly and softly that the interviewer
has difficulty catching all they say. You really must
speak in a clear, audible and as confident a voice as
possible. Remember also what we said a moment ago
about enthusiasm: let it show in your voice; you cannot
assert yourself very effectively if you are speaking in a
weary monotone, or in a nervous, hasty babble.

You can do too much talking sometimes, and this is
something to guard against. Do not let your answers
ramble on too long. Again, this is something you have
to judge for yourself, but a look at the interviewer's face
will sometimes give you a clue! The other point to
bring in here, though it has little to do with assertive
behaviour as such, is your accent. If you have a strong
regional, or even national, accent it may cross your
mind that it could be better to disguise it as best you
can. It is true that some interviewers react badly to
accents different from their own, but generally one has
too much else on one's mind in an interview to try and
talk in a different way as well. So be yourself, with the
exception only of someone who just does not seem to
understand what you are saying, in which case you may
need to speak a little more slowly.

Checking and clarifying

Some interviewees are very reluctant to interrupt an
interviewer, and generally this is quite right. However,
if the interviewer has clearly misunderstood what you
said in an answer to him, you should make that clear to

him. So do not be afraid to cut in if it is necessary to correct him. You can say something like 'I am sorry, that's not really what I meant.'

If you do not understand what the interviewer has asked, you should seek clarification rather than attempt an answer to what you think he might be asking. All you have to do is say something like 'I don't quite get your meaning', or 'I am not quite sure I understand the question.'

Arguing with the interviewer

Interviewees often wonder whether it is wise to disagree with an interviewer, even to argue with him. Well, it can go either way. Most interviewers seem to want applicants to be politely attentive and agreeable, but a few like to provoke applicants to see if they are able to look after themselves under stress. In general, it is best to avoid firm expressions of disagreement with interviewers, except where they get you to express your views on a topic and then present an opposing argument. This is quite common, the interviewer aiming to see how well you can argue a case and support your viewpoint. He may not himself actually believe the opposing views he puts to you, but he will play the role of devil's advocate if necessary. However, most exchanges are more like debates than arguments and the interviewer will remain friendly and business-like; there is little danger of mistaking this kind of exchange for one where the interviewer tries to provoke you or attack your views in a more personal way (in which case one often hears phrases like 'You don't mean to tell me that . . .', 'You are not seriously suggesting . . .', 'You seem to have made a bit of a mess of that', etc.) In similar vein, a few interviewers use sarcasm as a way of provoking the candidate, a lamentable strategy.

So, in general, do not look for arguments, but if one is 'offered' you should remain cool, defend your point of view in an agreeable way and be willing to acknowledge *some* sense in opposing views without actually accepting them.

Volunteering and seeking information

If you have prepared properly, you will know what information you want the interviewer to have about you at the end of the interview – the good points you have identified. Some of these will come out naturally in the course of a good interview, but the rest you need to feed in yourself. Answer questions in such a way that you can work into them the points *you* have decided you want to get across. You can also do a little gentle 'steering' of the discussion, e.g. if you are asked whether you ever go to the theatre, when in fact you are really much more keen and knowledgeable about the cinema, you need not just answer 'No' and hope that the interviewer will ask you about films. You can answer 'No, my interests are much more in the cinema; I go quite a lot; the interviewer will follow up from there. Do not miss opportunities of this kind for volunteering information on your strengths, and if no opportunity arises in respect of some of them, then you might be able to create it. For example, if you have some experience of working with computers which you feel is relevant to your application but which has not come out in the interview, you could introduce it by asking a question like 'Are there any opportunities for work in the computer field – I've already had some experience of that and enjoyed it.' The questions candidates are normally allowed to ask at the end of the interview offer a considerable opportunity to present any further information in this way.

Finally, do not voluntarily offer information on what you see as your weaker aspects. Apart from a tendency by some interviewers to give such negative points undue weight in their assessment, your idea of what is unsatisfactory may be at odds with the general standard of work (or whatever) in that area; in other words, you may be better than you think.

Helping the less competent interviewer

Many of the assertive forms of behaviour already mentioned will help interviewers who are not very good at their task. By helping them you will help yourself. So by all means expand on the closed questions they ask, instead of just answering very briefly. Give them plenty of leads to follow in your answers, and if they finally dry up, rescue them by saying something like 'Perhaps, to get a fuller picture of me, you ought to know about . . .', or 'Would it be helpful to you if I said something about . . .'. Also, if they fail to ask you if you want to ask questions of your own at the end of the interview, you can bring it to their notice that you would like to ask one or two things yourself. Less competent interviewers are usually grateful for candidates who gently take the initiative.

NON-VERBAL BEHAVIOUR

A great deal has been said and written about non-verbal behaviour, 'body language', expressive movement and so on. Certainly, the way we look and move can tell somebody else a lot about us, and often it gives a better guide to a person's feelings than what he actually says. The importance of non-verbal behaviour in the interview is, however, not altogether clear. Some research findings have indicated it as being an important part of the communication process, while others have shown it as having relatively little influence on the interaction between interviewer and candidate. To be on the safe side, I will assume here that it *can* affect interview judgements and will use the research findings to guide you as to what is and what is not advisable.

Some advice has already been given on this, in particular the desirability of smiling at the interviewer when you first meet him. However, the rest of what needs to be said can be dealt with under the headings of posture and eye contact.

Posture
This to some extent is dependent on the kind of chair you are given to sit in, but in general you should try to

sit comfortably and reasonably *upright* - no sprawling or slouching. As we said earlier, comfort is important to your relaxation in the interview, but it must not be at the expense of creating a lazy image. It is better to lean slightly *forward* than to lean back; it communicates interest and attentiveness (this works both ways - I have seen whole boards of interviewers visibly sway forward when an attractive female applicant walks into the room!).

An otherwise serene candidate often gives himself away by what he does with his hands and arms in an interview. Some grip the arms of the chair so tightly that their knuckles show white. Others gesticulate far too much, or continually shift the position of their arms. You can put your arms in just about any comfortable position, but do not keep shifting them; a lot of fidgeting seems to irritate some interviewers and is to be avoided. Also to be avoided is the habit of speaking with a hand in front of your mouth (playing with a beard, for instance) and any other mannerism that is likely to trigger off one of the interviewer's prejudices, e.g. head scratching, thumb picking, finger drumming.

So, as far as posture is concerned, the prescription is to keep fairly upright but leaning forward *slightly*, with low peripheral movement and as much relaxation as you can manage. You may like to find the most comfortable way of achieving this before you go for an interview, just place a chair in front of a mirror and see what position you feel most comfortable in while still meeting the requirements given above.

Eye contact
This term refers to occasions when two individuals are looking each other straight in the eye. Research has shown us quite a lot about patterns of eye contact and how they can influence our responses to one another. In normal conversation, the pattern is something like this. Individual A talks and sometimes looks (which means eye contact in this description) at individual B,

who listens and sometimes looks at A. When A stops talking, he looks at B, whereupon B generally averts his eyes from A while he plans his answer. When B commences his answer, he looks at A from time to time to see that A is attending and to note reactions, while A is listening and sometimes looking at B. This is more or less the pattern you will encounter in interviews. The next time you have a conversation with someone, try to notice how this pattern of eye contact works – it is a very consistent one. The important thing is that you *do* have eye contact with the interviewer. The amount of eye contact that takes place between people seems to be related to some extent to how much they like each other. This does not mean, however, that you must transfix the interviewer with an unwavering stare, as though you had never seen anything quite like it before. Look him in the eye when you first meet, look at him most of the time when he is talking and look at him some of the time when you are talking to him. The one thing not to do is to avoid the eyes of the interviewer most of the time.

If you are dealing with a board interview, face each interviewer as he or she questions you and again aim for a lot of eye contact. Also, occasionally glance at the other board members when you are replying, to show that your reply is to all of them and that you have not forgotten their presence.

THE INTERVIEWER'S BEHAVIOUR

The interview is very much a two-way communication process. The interviewer will be noting your behaviour (after all, that is what he is there for) and you will be noting his, sometimes mistakenly. Candidates are often quite strongly affected by what they see, or think they see, the interviewer doing during the course of the interview. Note-taking is a prime example. Many interviewers take notes during the interview, and very sensibly too as they will be hard pressed to remember everything they hear about a series of candidates. Unfortunately, some candidates get upset and think that something is wrong if the interviewer starts taking 'evidence' like this. In fact, you should be glad if notes are taken: the interviewer is doing his job properly! Another thing candidates pick up are the signals sometimes given to each other by different members of an interviewing board. All these should be ignored; they have no significance for the interviewee in terms of his assessment. The signals are usually to tell one board member that his allotted time questioning the candidate is up or almost up.

More disturbing for interviewees is the feedback they get from how the interviewer looks rather than anything he does. I stressed the importance of enthusiasm and interest on the part of the candidate a few pages ago. Well, the interviewer should really be able to project a little of this too, but he does not always do so. Often this is quite understandable as one interview follows another in what may be a period of days spent interviewing. Sometimes the interest, let alone energy and concentration, sags and the interviewer lets it show on his face. On no account must you let this deter you or dampen your own motivation. A persistent lack of enthusiasm from the interviewer is not necessarily an implied criticism of you – it usually stems from other things. Indeed, if the interviewer is fatigued or slightly bored with perhaps his fifth interview that day, it is all the more important that you do appear keen, interested and enthusiastic. Boredom and lack of interest breed boredom and lack of interest, but you cannot afford to let this happen.

CLOSING THE INTERVIEW

The final period of an interview is often the one used by interviewers to let you ask any questions you may have about the job or the organization, and you should have prepared these. Sometimes the interviewer will ask whether there is anything he has missed out or not asked you that he should; obviously, if there is anything else you feel may work to your credit that has not been covered, you will bring it up now. Even if you are not given this kind of opportunity by the interviewer, you can create it for yourself by saying something to the effect 'One thing that has not come out today and which you might find helpful to know is that I . . .'

Once again, as you say goodbye you should look the interviewer in the eye (or, if it is a board, a swift glance at each one of them) and smile. Sometimes the interviewer will offer a hand to shake, which you will of course take even though in some cases you will feel more like shaking him warmly by the throat!

SUMMARY OF ADVICE

The main points made in this chapter may be summarized in the form of a list of 'Do's' and Don'ts':

Do

Smile at the interviewer and look him in the eye when you meet and when you leave.

Maintain lots of eye-contact in the interview.

Sit upright and lean slightly forward.

Take your time in answering questions.

Look and sound both enthusiastic and interested.

Speak up.

Volunteer information that will help your case.

Try to help interviewers who are in difficulty.

Be willing to defend your viewpoint in a friendly way.

Do not

Slouch in the chair.

Fidget.

Panic if there is a period of silence.

Smoke (unless invited or unless really desperate) or chew anything.

Be evasive in your answers.

Boast or 'sell' yourself directly unless invited to.

Argue with the interviewer in any heated way.

Allow yourself to be put off if the interviewer seems unenthusiastic or bored.

7

The Use of Psychological Tests and Other Techniques

MULTIPLE PROCEDURES IN ASSESSMENT

We have seen that interviews are beset by problems and that they tend to be a rather poor way of selecting people for jobs. This has led to the search for other ways of comparing individuals and choosing between them. The interview will probably continue to be used for the reasons mentioned in Chapter 1, but increasingly it is being supplemented by other techniques. These include psychological tests of various kinds, group discussion tasks and certain objective performance measures on simulated work tasks. Sometimes all of these things may be used together in what is called an assessment centre procedure, something which is becoming more popular with organizations these days. The Civil Service Selection Board has actually been using a multiple procedure of this kind for many years and has a proven record of its effectiveness.

In this short chapter, I will try to describe some of the main kinds of supplementary assessment procedures you may encounter along with the interview. Apart from saying what they are, I will try to explain the main points about their use and, when appropriate, give some advice. The philosophy here, as in the case of interviews, is that they cause less anxiety for people who know what to expect and why they are being given.

THE USE OF PSYCHOLOGICAL TESTS

The use of these tests evokes strong emotional reactions from many people; some quite enjoy them while others seem to either fear them or ridicule them (or both). Much of the abuse hurled at them is extremely ill-informed, which is not really surprising since psychological testing is a far more complex and sophisticated field than it appears on the surface. The value of these tests in predicting success in work settings is well established, and their use is increasing; they are here to stay because they work reasonably well.

As long as the psychological test is properly used, you have no reason to fear it. Selection decisions are seldom based on test data alone, and the test data can sometimes help offset a bad interview performance, (though it seldom seems to work in the other direction you will be glad to know). The best general advice one can give is to urge you to get some *practice* at taking tests. This will make relatively little difference to your performance of them under non-stressful circumstances (practice on IQ tests only raises scores a limited amount), but it may make quite a lot of difference to the way you *feel* if you have to take such tests as part of a selection procedure. That is rather more stressful, and the phenomenon of test anxiety rears its head; your performance can suffer through anxiety, so that you do not give a fair impression of your ability. However, if you have previously worked through examples of the kind of test items you are likely to encounter, you will probably feel much happier and more confident about them. Two books which may well help in this respect are *Know your own IQ* by H. J. Eysenck and *Know your own personality* by Glen Wilson and H. J. Eysenck (both published by Penguin). These contain plenty of examples of items typical of IQ and personality tests.

Tests of intelligence take many different forms according to the aspect of intelligence being assessed, the characteristics of the group being assessed and the purposes of the assessment. The variation in the content of these tests is so great that any proper discussion of them is beyond the scope of this book. But one important point you should keep in mind about them is that they can be of some help to you if you are lacking in formal academic or other qualifications. Often an intelligence test will indicate that someone who has few exam passes is really very bright, thus directing the interviewers toward finding out why the educational attainment was low relative to the individual's potential as shown by the tests. In this way, test data can offset some of the disadvantages of a poor or deprived background by giving a clearer picture of a person's ability than do his school attainments. Many tests can do this because they are thought to measure basic reasoning power; they may include non-verbal items that do not rely on how well an individual has been taught English or Mathematics (at home or at school). On the debit side, however, it must also be admitted that some psychological tests have a cultural bias that can in some cases put members of minority racial groups at a disadvantage (though this can to an extent be offset by the length of time the individual has lived in a Western culture).

Turning to personality tests, one must first make it clear that a psychologist's use of the term personality is not the same as the layman's; the psychological concept of personality does not involve ideas about one person having more personality than another, or one person having a better or worse personality than someone else. In personality tests there are no 'right' answers as such. The replies are used to give a picture of the individual's enduring traits, dispositions and motives. Again, there

are many types of personality test. The most frequently
encountered is the questionnaire type which takes the
person's reply on anything from 50 to 500 questions
and processes them in such a way as to yield scores on
various traits or other aspects of personality. Less often
encountered is the projective type of personality test.
This is where you are presented with an ambiguous or
abstract stimulus, e.g. an ink-blot or a picture of some
domestic scene, and asked to say something about it (in
the case of an ink-blot, what it reminds you of; in the
case of a picture, make up a story about what is
happening). The idea is that in responding, you
'project' important aspects of your personality in your
interpretation of the stimulus. However, there are
serious problems associated with the use of projective
tests and their value as selection devices is highly
questionable except in a small minority of rather
special cases.

TAKING THE TESTS

There is little else that can be said in regard to
intelligence tests. *Always* read the instructions carefully - do not hurry over them. If you are taking a test
that is timed, you have to work out your own strategy:
working quickly and increasing the chance of errors or
working more slowly with less chance of errors but less
chance of completing the test too. As a general rule it is
not good to go so slowly that many items are not
attempted. What you can do is to leave any items which
cause you particular difficulty until you have completed the rest and then return to them if you have any
time left. When you are actually doing the tests
concentrate on the task in hand, and try to ignore any
other job applicants who may be taking the same tests
as you (they are often administered to groups of people
together), or you may start worrying if they seem to be
working much more quickly than you or acting
differently in any other way. Do *not* concern yourself
with them, or whether they are doing better than you,

simply get on with the task in hand and keep your head down!

Personality tests are a different matter altogether. They are usually open to a number of distorting influences, an important one being social desirability. This is the tendency some people show to answer questions in the way that they think will put them in the best light: answering questions in the 'right' way. This may or may not be a conscious phenomenon, but it is certainly a real one. Related to this is the more serious problem of deliberate faking. People have different ideas of what personality questionnaires are measuring and of what 'sort' of personality the organization is trying to recruit; they sometimes try to present themselves on such questionnaires in the way that will increase their chances of acceptance rather than in the way that will give the truest picture of their personality. Many studies have shown that job applicants are sometimes less than truthful when doing personality tests. Even psychiatric patients diagnosed as schizophrenic can manipulate the impression they give of themselves on these devices, so it is not surprising that psychologically normal individuals are prone to do so as well; some writers have even given advice on the kind of personality it is safest to project on tests. For example, William Whyte Jr in his famous book *The organization man* suggested all applicants taking personality tests should repeat the following to themselves:

> I loved my father and my mother, but my father a little bit more. I like things pretty much the way they are. I never worry much about anything. I do not care for books or music much. I love my wife and children. I do not let them get in the way of company work.

Clearly the idea is to present as conventional an image as possible. While this advice from Whyte is quite amusing and contains some sense, it is also a little dangerous. Not all jobs or organizations need or seek the same kind of personality profile. Guessing the kind of personality characteristics a company is seeking from its applicants is a hazardous business because of the wide difference between them on some things. Moreover, most personality tests contain special items for detecting people who are either showing social desirability, effects or blatantly faking. Some of these 'lie scores' and other devices are fairly easy to spot, but many are not. They are thus another danger for anyone trying to deliberately present himself in a particular way that he thinks will go down well. All in all, honesty probably remains the best policy on personality tests.

OTHER SELECTION TECHNIQUES

When appointing people to senior posts, or to posts which probably will in time lead on to quite senior jobs, it is increasingly common to find that the candidates are observed and assessed actually performing a range of tasks. The qualities to be noted from these exercises are specified beforehand as being relevant to the job and often cover things that are felt to be inadequately assessed by the interview alone, e.g. leadership, ability to influence others, administrative skills.

The most frequent technique of this type is to put anything from four to eight candidates together in a group and give them one or more topics to discuss as a group. Often they have to come to a group decision or solution to a problem posed. While the candidates are discussing the topic provided, observers sit round the outside of them and note each individual's contribution to the discussion. It would not be appropriate to reveal precisely what aspects of behaviour are assessed (they vary anyway) in these settings, but obviously they relate to an individual's functioning as a member of a work group.

Another approach that is growing in popularity is

the 'In-tray' exercise. This consists of a series of documents designed to resemble the kind of paperwork problems that managers in those organizations would encounter very frequently. The candidates are usually given some time to study background details of the organization before tackling the problems and taking appropriate action within the time allowed. Their handling of these tasks is rated on various aspects of effectiveness.

Finally, some selection procedures involve candidates in group tasks of a more physical nature. This is particularly true of officer selection in the armed forces. A typical task would be for a group of candidates, with one designated as leader, to have to manoeuvre a heavy object over a series of obstacles with the aid of only rudimentary equipment (generally the candidates have to produce some novel ideas on how to utilize this equipment to achieve the target set).

All of these procedures focus on certain aspects of behaviour more closely than does the interview, and the value of the assessments made from them can be considerable. They may tell you less overall about a person, but what they do tell you is more specific, easier to relate to particular facets of the job being applied for and generally more reliable as a form of evidence. The best results are obtained, as indicated at the beginning of this chapter when one or more of these procedures are used in conjunction with the interview and the information from all the different sources pooled for the final decision.

8

Reviewing Your Performance

ANALYSING AND INTERPRETING THE INTERVIEW

We learn best from experience, and to get the most out of your experience of interviews you need to analyse and interpret them as soon afterwards as possible (otherwise your memory will obscure much of the detail). Do not wait until you hear the outcome of your application, because quite apart from the likelihood of forgetting what went on, your later perceptions of the interview may be highly coloured by your acceptance or rejection. So think about it within 24 hours. To help you do this in a fairly structured way, you might like to use the following review guide:

What do you feel your chances of success are?
What were you overall reactions? What sort of experience was it - enjoyable, tense, unpleasant, challenging, or what?
Did the interviewers seem friendly and interested?
Was the interview fairly and competently conducted? If not, what do you think they should have done differently, and why?

Did you manage to stay (or at least, *appear*) relaxed and confident in manner?

What topics were covered? (Write down all that you can remember as soon as you can after the interview.)

Which of them had you anticipated, and which came as unexpected?

What did you feel you put across well? What do you feel you could have improved upon, and how?

Were there any questions you found particularly difficult? Why?

How did you cope with them?

What sort of impression do you feel you made on the interviewer(s)?

What did you learn from this interview about presenting yourself?

If you need to go for further interviews, what aspects of your interview performance will you try to improve, and how?

Having answered all the above questions and thought about them, is your answer to the first question in this list still the same?

If you think about these questions in relation to your interview, you should reap considerable benefit from it as a learning experience. And as far as this is concerned, it really does not matter whether the interview turns out to be a successful one for you or not; even if you find you have been appointed, there will be other interviews in the future, either for promotion or when you change jobs.

THE OUTCOME OF THE INTERVIEW

If you get the job, little more needs to be said, apart from congratulating you (do not forget to let your referees know, and thank them). However, few people get what they are after with just one interview. You have to accept that no matter how well you do in both preparing and presenting yourself, someone else may have done just as well and have formal qualifications superior to your own. Not being offered a job should not be taken as a reproach; it is inevitable that a lot of people interviewed as part of a given selection process will not get jobs, because more are interviewed than there are vacancies. There is no disgrace (as some people give the impression of feeling) in admitting that some people are better suited or better qualified for a job than you are. Besides which, some candidates are rejected because they are too *good* for the job!

So there is certainly no point in blaming yourself unless you just did not bother to prepare for the interview and took a passive role in it. Taking steps to improve your chances next time is much more constructive. Reviewing your performance is one important activity that has already been mentioned. Another possible measure is to actually contact the interviewer, usually by writing a *polite* letter, though sometimes by phone if you think he would not mind, and asking him what it was about your application or interview performance that let you down, if anything (someone might just have been better). Where the interview concerned was one of a considerable number carried out as part of a large-scale recruitment exercise, you probably would not be able to do this. But in many other cases it is worth a try and can sometimes provide useful feedback, though one should treat what is said with some caution as the interviewer may not be entirely frank in his comments or may simply have made his decision to reject you on poor grounds. Another word of warning; be careful when phoning or writing to the interviewer that you do not in any way give the impression of asking him to 'justify' a selection decision which you feel aggrieved at.

Failing to get a job from two or three interviews should not cause alarm or despondency, but if the lack of success continues much beyond that, it may call for a more fundamental reappraisal. Clearly, if you have been getting the interviews then you are definitely in the running as far as the organization is concerned. So what is going wrong? It may be that you are applying for jobs where the competition is particularly intense and where it would be quite common to find people having numerous interviews before being 'lucky' (and there is often an element of luck in interviews). On the other hand, you may be putting yourself over in the interview just as well as anyone else but not striking the interviewers as being the right type of person for this type of job, and they may be right. So, after a prolonged period without success you should, perhaps, think of getting some expert advice from a careers officer or from a private vocational counselling practitioner. Ideally, you would have been given this sort of help in the first place, but this is all too rarely the case. Better late than never, though, and seeking guidance after a series of rejections might well throw some new light on the problem and lead to a better fit between your qualities and skills and the requirements of the jobs you apply for.

The majority of readers of this book are unlikely to experience repeated rejections; the very fact that you have read it suggests that you are approaching the business of seeking the job you want with commitment and vigour. The effort you are putting in now will be repaid many times over when you find the right job. You have taken in a lot of advice in the course of reading through this book, and if you combine it with something much more important – namely, your own wit and intelligence – you will be in a position to tackle the all important interview in the positive manner it needs for success.

APPENDIX

Interview Preparation Programme and Checklist

(a) Obtain details and background information about the organization concerned. Find out anything you can about their method of selecting people, and about the kinds of questions they ask in interviews.

(b) Visit the place where the interviews will be held if this is not too far away. Apart from getting the feel of the place and collecting any background literature available, you can check the transport arrangements when doing this dry-run.

(c) Be sure you know how to get to the interview location (ideally by the method outlined above). Look at the relevant timetables for transport and arrange things so that you have an adequate safety margin if any delays occur.

(d) Remember to present as neat, clean and tidy an appearance as possible (wash your hair, get your clothes cleaned, etc.).

(e) Re-read the copy of the application form if you have kept one.

(f) Work through the questions listed below.

QUESTION PREPARATION

The questions listed below are frequently asked in interviews, though not always in quite the form given here. For the purposes of the present exercise, some questions that are related and would come (during an interview) in a sequence have been run together. Also you should note that whether a question is put in the past tense or present tense is irrelevant; simply take it as being in the tense that applies to you (e.g. when a question about your college course is worded as if you have left when in fact you are still at college). The actual wording of the questions in the interview may be different from that given here, but the information and thought required from you will be much the same.

The questions have been put under a few headings representing the main topic areas as described in Chapters 4 and 5. Inevitably, some of this categorising is arbitrary and some of the questions could come under any of several headings as they provide information about them. Work through the questions slowly. Not *all* of them will apply to everyone, of course, so use your own sense in identifying those not relevant to you. Some very basic, mundane questions have been included and these will take very little time to deal with. However, the trickier questions deserve more time and consideration. With each one you should first think about the information asked for and then consider how to put it across, with the accent on a *positive* approach. Consider how your answers might be received by other people.

Now, before you start going through the questions, do the following tasks by way of a complementary exercise:

(a) Write a description of yourself as though through a friend's eyes; then write one as might be produced by someone critical of you.

(b) Write down a list of the abilities, qualifications, personal qualities and experience that you think would be called for to do well the job you are applying for.

Having done these two things, work through the questions.

FAMILY BACKGROUND

What does your father do for a living?
Does your mother work? If so, what does she do?
Have you any brothers or sisters? Older or younger than you? Do they work, and if so, what do they do?
What is/was life like at home?
Did you spend your childhood in one area, or did you move around a lot?
If you did move around, what effect (if any) did this have on you?
How did your parents feel about (a) you staying on/leaving school, (b) going to college, (c) applying for this kind of job.
What influence have your parents had on the decisions you have taken in your life?
If you no longer live at home now, how did you feel about leaving home?
Are you thinking of getting married in the near future?

EDUCATION AND TRAINING

The first five questions apply to both school and college or university:

What did you think of it? What did you like best about the place, and what least? Why?
What subjects (or parts of them) were you best at, and why? Which subjects were you least good at, and why?
What subjects did you *like* best? Why? Which subjects did you *like* least? Why?
What guided your choice of subjects/courses?
Do your examination results fairly reflect your ability? If not, give your reasons for believing they do not.
Why did you stay on at school (or, why did you not stay on)?
Why did you/did you not choose to go to college?

Did you consider any alternatives to continuing your education? Why did you reject them?

Why did you go to that particular college?

What do you think of the course? How could it be improved?

What do you think of this country's system of higher education? Would you make any changes in it – if so, what and why?

Did you do any special projects at college? Describe them, briefly.

Have you done any postgraduate or other research work? If so, describe in terms that a non-specialist could understand.

(In relation to any college projects or postgraduate work.) What implications do the results have? What applications does the work have? What relevance does it have for this job and the kind of work it involves?

What did you get out of your time at college?

Do you pursue any educational courses in your own time?

Do you speak any foreign languages? How well?

WORK EXPERIENCE

In regard to any full-time job, and also some part-time jobs, the following questions can come up:

How/why did you come to take this job?

What did *your particular* job entail – what did you actually have to do?

What skills/qualities were needed?

What did you like and dislike about it? Why?

Were you good at it? If not, why?

How would you have improved the job, given the chance?

What was the most difficult aspect of it?

What problems did you encounter? How did you tackle them?

How did you get on with your colleagues?

What did you get out of the job? What did you learn from it? How does it relate to the job you are applying for now – what help would it be to you?

Why did you leave?/Why do you want to leave?

Have you any experience of managing staff? If so, give details.
If not, how do you feel you would cope with it?
Have you done any figure work (accounts, etc.) in your jobs? Do you like that sort of work? How good are you with figures?
Do you know much about computers? Have you any experience of working with them?

MOTIVATION AND ASPIRATION

What do you know about this organization, and about its products or services?
Who is the head man or woman in it?
Has this organization been in the news at all recently?
Have any developments (social, economic, political, scientific or technological) of the recent past got any particular implications for this organization and its products or services? If so, what are they?
Why do you want this job? What appeals to you about it?
Has anyone given you any advice that helped persuade you to apply for this? Who?
What alternatives to this job are you considering, if any?
If you have considered some and rejected them, why?
Which part of the organization's function are you most interested in? Why?
Are you willing to move to another part of the country if the firm needs to send you there?
Would you want a job that involves a lot of travelling round?
How would you feel about working irregular hours or overtime if required?
Why do you think you will be good at this job? What evidence can you point to in support of this?
What are your strengths and weaknesses?
What do you want out of a job?
How do you see your career developing over the next few years?
What do you think you will do if you do not get this particular job?

The following questions come broadly in the same area of motivation and aspiration, but concentrate more directly on your personality and attitudes.

Who and what have been the main influences in your life? Why?

Have you ever been under any stress? How did you cope?

Would you say you were a competitive person or not? What evidence have you for your answer?

Are you more of a 'team' member or an individualist? Are you ambitious?

What sort of people do you get on with best? Why?

What sort of people do you find it most difficult to get on with? Why?

Have most of the people you have met in your life come from much the same kind of background as yourself, or have they been from lots of very different backgrounds?

Are you a gregarious person?

What would you do if given a completely free choice (say, through winning a fortune)?

This is the end of the list of questions. Having gone through them and thought about each one, look back at the two things you were asked to do before you started. Are there any changes you would make to the 'friend' and 'critic' descriptions of yourself? Any additions or alterations to them? And in relation to the abilities, qualities, experience and qualifications you feel are needed for the job – how do you feel you match up now that you have answered the questions above? Does this seem the right kind of job for you? Make a list of what you have to offer in parallel with what the job seems to demand, and from that identify the strengths and weaknesses in your application; how can you emphasize the strengths in an interview, and what can you offer to compensate for the weaknesses?